Contents

D1419677

Chronology

1921
Northern Ireland state established.
1922-24
Internment without trial in operation.
1932
Unemployment riots in Belfast.
1933
Special Powers Act made permanent.
1935
Sectarian riots in Belfast.
1938-45
Small-scale IRA campaign. Internment without trial in operation.
1956-62
IRA Border campaign. Internment without trial in operation.

> **1959** Cuban revolution.
> **1960** Sharpeville massacre in South Africa. Sit-ins and "freedom rides" in US southern states.
> **1962** French leave Algeria. Cuban missile crisis.

1963
Terence O'Neill succeeds Lord Brookeborough as N. Ireland Prime Minister.

> Martin Luther King leads civil rights march on Washington DC.

1964
JANUARY. Campaign for Social Justice set up.
OCTOBER. Riots in Divis Street, Belfast.

> OCTOBER. Labour government elected in Britain.

1965
JANUARY. Sean Lemass, head of Dublin government, meets O'Neill.

> JANUARY. US troops intervene in Vietnam.
> MARCH. US civil rights march from Selma to Montgomery in Alabama.

1966
MARCH. Labour government re-elected in Britain. Gerry Fitt elected MP for West Belfast.
MAY/JUNE. Three die in UVF attacks in Belfast.

1967

JANUARY.   Northern Ireland Civil Rights Association set up.

MARCH.   Republican Clubs banned; Queen's University students march in protest.

OCTOBER.   Che Guevara killed in Bolivia.

NOVEMBER.   1,500 students protest at Republican Clubs ban.

1968

FEBRUARY.   Tet offensive in Vietnam. "Prague spring" in Czechoslovakia.

MARCH.   Italian students fight police in Rome.

APRIL.   Martin Luther King assassinated.

MAY.   Student revolt in Paris; French General Strike.

JUNE/JULY.   Housing protest in Caledon, County Tyrone.

AUGUST.   Riots at US Democratic Party Convention in Chicago. Soviet invasion of Czechoslovakia.

AUGUST.   Civil rights march from Coalisland to Dungannon, County Tyrone.

OCTOBER.   Civil rights march in Derry. Student march in Belfast; Peoples Democracy formed.

OCTOBER.   300 students killed by police in Mexico on eve of Olympic Games.

NOVEMBER.   Mass civil rights march in Derry. O'Neill announces reform package.

DECEMBER.   O'Neill calls for moratorium on marches.

1969

JANUARY.   Peoples Democracy' march from Belfast to Derry.

FEBRUARY.   Stormont election: John Hume and other "moderate" civil rights leaders elected; Peoples Democracy get 23,645 votes.

APRIL.   Peoples Democracy' march to Dublin. Bernadette Devlin elected MP. O'Neill resigns, replaced by James Chichester-Clark.

AUGUST.   Battle of the Bogside in Derry; attack on Catholic ghettos in Belfast. British troops intervene. Jack Lynch's "we will not stand (idly) by" speech.

SEPTEMBER.   Government-appointed Cameron Commission confirms civil rights grievances.

OCTOBER.   Millions in US demonstrate against Vietnam war.

OCTOBER.   Disbandment of B Specials announced; loyalists riot in Belfast and kill RUC man.

1970

IRA and Sinn Féin split; Provisional IRA formed.

APRIL. US troops enter Cambodia. National Guard kill four students at Kent State college.

MAY. Arms Crisis in Republic; Charles Haughey and Neil Blaney sacked from Cabinet and charged with importing arms.

JUNE. Conservative government elected in Britain.

JUNE. Provisional IRA involved in gun battles in Belfast.

JULY. Curfew and major arms search in Falls area of Belfast.

AUGUST. SDLP formed.

1971

FEBRUARY. First British soldier killed by Provisionals; bombing and shooting campaign escalates.

MARCH. Chichester-Clark resigns, succeeded by Brian Faulkner.

AUGUST. Internment without trial introduced. Rent and rates strike against internment.

1972

JANUARY. Bloody Sunday: British soldiers kill 13 protesters in Derry; British embassy burned in Dublin.

MARCH. Stormont government suspended.

JUNE/JULY. Provisional IRA ceasefire and talks with British government.

JULY. Ceasefire ends. British army ends nationalist "no go" areas.

DECEMBER. Non-jury "Diplock" courts announced.

1973

FEBRUARY. Fine Gael/Labour Party coalition government elected in Republic.

JUNE. Election to new N. Ireland Assembly: SDLP wins 19 seats out of 78; Peoples Democracy and Sinn Féin boycott election.

JUNE. US troops withdraw from Vietnam.

DECEMBER. Sunningdale conference of British and Irish governments; Unionists, SDLP and Alliance Party agree on power-sharing Executive in N. Ireland, with SDLP participation, and a Council of Ireland.

1974

FEBRUARY. Labour government elected in Britain. Hard-line Unionists defeat moderates; Bernadette (Devlin) McAliskey defeated.

MAY. Loyalist work stoppage; power-sharing Executive collapses.

JULY. Watergate: Nixon resigns as US President.

NOVEMBER. IRA bombs in Birmingham kill 21 people. Prevention of Terrorism Act introduced.

DECEMBER. Dissident members of Official Sinn Féin set up Irish Republican Socialist Party/Irish National Liberation Army.

1975

JANUARY. IRA truce with British government.

MAY. Election to N. Ireland Convention; hard-line Unionists win majority.

APRIL. Vietnamese National Liberation Front captures Saigon.

NOVEMBER. British authorities formally end truce.

DECEMBER. Last internees released.

1976

MARCH. Special category status abolished for future prisoners in N. Ireland.

SEPTEMBER. First IRA prisoner begins "blanket" protest for political status. Fair Employment Agency set up.

1977

JUNE. Fianna Fáil government elected in Republic.

1978 JANUARY. European Court of Human Rights finds Britain guilty of "inhuman and degrading treatment" of 12 internees.

MARCH. H Block prisoners begin "dirty protest".

1979

JANUARY. Burntollet anniversary march.

MARCH. Government-commissioned Bennett Report finds prisoners have been seriously injured in RUC custody.

MAY. Conservative government elected in Britain.

JUNE. EEC election: Ian Paisley, John Hume and J. Taylor (Un.) elected; Bernadette (Devlin) McAliskey gets 33,969 votes in support of protesting prisoners.

JULY. Sandinistas take power in Nicaragua

1980

OCTOBER. H Block prisoners go on hunger strike for political status.

DECEMBER. Hunger strike ends.

1981

MARCH. Second hunger strike begins.

APRIL. Hunger striker Bobby Sands elected to Westminster.

MAY.   Bobby Sands and three other hunger strikers die.

JUNE.   Fine Gael/Labour Party coalition government elected in Republic; two H Block prisoners elected to the Dáil.

AUGUST.   Owen Carron elected to Westminster, succeeding Bobby Sands.

OCTOBER.   Hunger strike ends with ten dead.

NOVEMBER.   IRA member Christopher Black becomes first "supergrass".

1982

NOVEMBER.   N. Ireland Assembly elections: Sinn Féin stand and get 10% of the vote; SDLP 19%.

NOVEMBER/DECEMBER.   RUC shoot dead six unarmed men in "shoot to kill" incidents in County Armagh.

1983

MAY.   New Ireland Forum involving Southern parties and SDLP set up.

JUNE.   Conservative government re-elected in Britain. John Hume elected for Derry, Gerry Adams for West Belfast; SDLP get 137,012 votes, Sinn Féin 102,701.

SEPTEMBER.   Referendum in Republic enacts constitutional ban on abortion.

> SEPTEMBER.   Campaign against job discrimination in N. Ireland begins in US.

1984

JUNE.   EEC election: Paisley, Hume, Taylor re-elected; Sinn Féin vote drops by 11,000.

> JUNE.   MacBride Principles against discrimination in N. Ireland drafted in US.

1985

JANUARY.   New York City Council becomes first US public body to endorse MacBride Principles.

MAY.   N. Ireland local elections: Sinn Féin win 59 seats.

NOVEMBER.   Anglo-Irish Agreement signed: London and Dublin to consult on N. Ireland policy.

1986

JANUARY.   By-elections for N. Ireland seats at Westminster: Seamus Mallon (SDLP) wins seat; Sinn Féin vote drops.

JUNE.   Referendum on divorce in Republic: 63.5% vote to keep constitutional ban.

NOVEMBER.   Sinn Féin vote to drop abstention from Dáil.

1987

JUNE.   Conservative government re-elected in Britain. SDLP win three seats, Sinn Féin one.

OCTOBER.   Standing Advisory Commission on Human Rights in N. Ireland reports Catholic male unemployment two and a half times rate for Protestants; no improvement over last decade.

NOVEMBER.   IRA bomb kills eleven in Enniskillen.

DECEMBER.   New extradition law in Republic abolishes protection for political offenders.

1988

JANUARY.   John Hume and Gerry Adams meet to start talks between SDLP and Sinn Féin. For reasons of Britain's "national security" RUC men accused of conspiracy to pervert the course of justice in 1982 "shoot to kill" incidents not to be prosecuted. British Court of Appeal rejects plea by Birmingham Six.

FEBRUARY.   John Stalker's book on his inquiry into the "shoot to kill" cases published. Unarmed man shot dead at British army checkpoint at Aughnacloy, County Tyrone. First British soldier jailed for killing civilian while on duty released after serving 26 months of jail sentence and reinstated in army.

MARCH.   SAS shoot dead three unarmed IRA members in Gibraltar. British government's new fair employment plans widely criticised as inadequate. Loyalist gunman kills three people at IRA funeral in Belfast; two British soldiers killed at funeral of one of gunman's victims.

JUNE.   Amnesty International report expresses concern that there may have been a policy "to eliminate ... members of armed opposition groups" in N. Ireland and calls for judicial inquiry into killings.

INTRODUCTION

Che Guevara was killed by the military regime in Bolivia in October 1967. Pictures of his body displayed like a trophy by the Bolivian army were flashed around the world. If they were meant to inspire fear and deter others, they had the opposite effect. The heroic story of the Argentinian revolutionary, who fought alongside Fidel Castro in the Cuban revolution and then set off to find new peoples to free, moved a whole generation of youth across the world.

We had already been inspired by Martin Luther King's "I have a dream" speech at a massive civil rights march in Washington in 1963, and angered at newsreel pictures of racist United States police batoning black protesters in America's southern states. We had wept at film of children burned by napalm in Vietnam. And Bob Dylan and Joan Baez had expressed our anger and frustration.

Revolution was in the air in the late '60s. There were many factors behind the change, but probably the main one was the relative boom in the 1960s after 15-20 years of post-Second World War austerity. The struggle to live was no longer so grinding. There were more jobs — at least in Europe and America — and there was more money about. Young people were less dependent than ever before on their elders and were more confident and assertive and less respectful of authority. Lifestyles were changing from the narrow, socially and sexually repressive '50s. The contraceptive pill paved the way for a sexual revolution. Greater prosperity meant that women were encouraged to work outside the home and be independent. There was a huge expansion in higher education. Young people began to question and challenge

tastes and conventions in music, clothes, appearance, sexual mores
— everything. And television made the world a global village so
that the new music, new styles and new ideas spread like wildfire.
There was a tremendous sense of liberation from old hide-bound
attitudes. New cults and theories flourished; hippies, beatniks
and freaks of all kinds prospered.

But television also brought home the injustices in the world:
the Sharpeville massacre by South African police in 1960; the
tortures inflicted by the French army during the Algerian war of
independence; the horrors of Vietnam. And we grew up under
the shadow of the atom bomb. Gradually information seeped out
about the scale and horror of the casualties at Hiroshima and
Nagasaki while the Cold War threatened to unleash a nuclear
holocaust at any time. For a few days during the Cuban missile
crisis in October 1962 — my first term at Queen's University,
Belfast — it looked as if the holocaust was about to start. A lot of
young people in the West were bitterly resentful of the world
they had inherited: a world divided into rich and poor, even
within the advanced countries; a world disfigured by racism and
colonialism, and threatened with extinction by the Cold War and
the policy of nuclear deterrence. But for a long time they had
felt hopeless about it and could see no road to change. The
communist regimes in Eastern Europe had become bureaucratic,
brutal and repressive. A whole generation of communists had
had their illusions shattered when Soviet tanks crushed a workers'
uprising in Hungary in 1956.

By the beginning of the '60s that too had begun to change.
Fidel Castro's ragged army of guerrillas had toppled Cuba's
corrupt, US-backed dictatorship in 1959 and beaten off a US-
supported invasion in 1961. Defending their tiny island right in
America's backyard, the bearded Fidel and his charismatic
lieutenant Che Guevara became symbols to rebellious youth all
over the world — all the more so when Che began outlining a
new socialist humanism very different from the drab
bureaucratism of Eastern Europe. On the other side of the world
the Algerian rebels won their independence in 1962 after an
eight-year war, while Cyprus and a number of the British and
French colonies in Africa became independent at the end of the
'50s and the beginning of the 1960s. And the "freedom rides"
and sit-ins by civil rights activists protesting against racial
segregation in America's southern states began in 1960. The old
colonial empires appeared to be breaking up and protest and

resistance was spreading to the very heart of the capitalist world. It spread wider in 1965 when US troops were sent to Vietnam and leftist protesters were joined by college students resisting conscription to fight Uncle Sam's war in South-East Asia.

To the more politicised of the '60s generation — those who wanted political and social as well as cultural change — things no longer seemed hopeless: imperialist powers could be beaten or forced to retreat after all. And the choice now was not just between Western capitalism and East European Stalinism; there was also Che's humanistic socialism. The writings of Leon Trotsky, who had opposed Stalin's dictatorship in the Soviet Union, were rediscovered. In China, from 1965 on, students advocating a cultural revolution appeared to be shaking the whole bureaucracy to the core. We believed that our generation could change the world and that students could be the catalysts in setting off a social and political revolution.

In 1968 it all boiled over. In February the Vietnamese staged the Tet offensive, a heroic, if suicidal, uprising that captured the old imperial capital of their country at Hue and brought guerrilla fighters inside the perimeter of the US embassy in Saigon. It showed the world that all America's might could not crush a small Asian nation fighting for its freedom. In Czechoslovakia the Stalinist monolith began to break up in the "Prague spring", when a new reforming leadership in the Communist Party sparked off an avalanche of democratic meetings and students' and workers' action committees. In March Italian students fought a five-hour battle with police in the streets of Rome. In April Martin Luther King was assassinated in Memphis, Tennessee, where he had gone to support a black garbage workers' strike, and black America erupted in revolt. In May students in Paris revolted, sparking off a general strike which nearly brought down the government of General de Gaulle.

The turmoil continued. During the summer Japanese students clad in their own riot gear fought pitched battles with the police in anti-American protests. In August US police savagely attacked anti-Vietnam war protesters outside the Democratic Party Convention in Chicago. Later the same month Soviet tanks invaded Czechoslovakia and students and young workers fought back with their bare hands. One student, Jan Palach, burned himself to death in the centre of Prague in protest. In October in Mexico city troops and police killed 300 students on the eve of the Olympic games. They were protesting about the poverty and slum housing in the city.

In the early 1960s, by contrast, Queen's University, Belfast, had been one of the most docile campuses in Western Europe. There was a handful of radicals, not more than 15 or 20 in number. Young people in general in the city were no better than Queen's students. We could never muster more than a dozen for an anti-apartheid picket or 50 for a CND march. The intellectual ferment, the revolution in manners and morals, had barely reached our shores. But there were stirrings beneath the surface and in 1967 things began to change. International events were beginning to have their effect. The student body was changing too as a result of the post-Second World War education acts. There were more students now and they were less privileged. There were still not many from the working class, but more from the lower middle class. And there were more from Northern Ireland's Catholic minority and numbers gave them more confidence to voice their opinions. In 1967 Queen's University students staged their first significant protest march — against a Northern Ireland government ban on Republican Clubs, a new attempt by the banned republican party, Sinn Féin, to go legitimate. By October 1968 students at Queen's University were ready to play a part, however small, in the worldwide revolt of their generation. And circumstances in Northern Ireland were about to give them the opportunity to do so; and in a way that would have a more profound and lasting effect than any of the other student revolts in that year of revolutions. Because in 1968 the long pent-up frustrations of the Catholic/nationalist population of Northern Ireland at last came to a head.

The Northern Ireland state had been set up in 1921 against the wishes of the majority of the Irish population and of a one third minority within its own borders. It was based on a simple sectarian headcount — a majority of Protestants/Unionists and a minority of Catholics/nationalists — and it was set up by force, using a draconian Special Powers Act and a wholly Protestant militia called the Ulster Special Constabulary to suppress nationalist resistance. Once in power the new Ulster Unionist regime did not concede an inch to the defeated minority. For 50 years no Catholic was ever a member of the Northern Ireland government, or even of the ruling party in the Northern parliament at Stormont, and local government boundaries were gerrymandered to prevent Catholics/nationalists from exercising control even at local level. The worst example was Derry City, which had to be re-gerrymandered twice to control an ever-growing Catholic majority. And the regime institutionalised an already prevalent system of religious discrimination in jobs and housing that left Catholics/nationalists (for most practical purposes the Unionist authorities regarded the terms as synonymous) as second-class citizens.

Catholics were excluded from the public service or kept on the lowest rung of the ladder. In 1934 the English-born head of the Northern Ireland civil service, himself a strong Unionist, was so irritated by the constant pressure to exclude Catholics that he said: "If the Prime Minister is dissatisfied with our present system, I think the only course would be for the government to come out in the open and say that only Protestants are admitted to the service".[1] And four years later an internal report by the British government's Dominions Office noted that "there can be little doubt that in those areas where there is a Protestant majority on the (local government) council, in practice posts do not often go to Catholics".[2] Discrimination was also rife in the private sector, and received official Unionist encouragement. In July 1933 Sir Basil Brooke, a junior minister in the Belfast government, having pointed out that "he had not a Roman Catholic about his own place", appealed to loyalists "wherever possible, to employ good Protestant lads and lassies". The following year the Prime Minister, Lord Craigavon, endorsed Brooke's call,[3] and within ten years Brooke himself was Prime Minister. Many of the large employers followed his advice and Catholics were virtually excluded from the shipbuilding industry — Northern Ireland's biggest employer — and from the skilled engineering trades.

By the late '60s discrimination had become a way of life in Northern Ireland. A study based on the 1971 census figures

1. W.B. Spender, head of Northern Ireland civil service, to C.H. Blackmore, Cabinet Secretary, 8 November 1934, quoted in Fair Employment Agency for Northern Ireland, *Report of an investigation by the Fair Employment Agency for Northern Ireland into the non-industrial Northern Ireland Civil Service.* Belfast: FEA 1983, Appendix IV.
2. Report by Sir H.F. Batterbee on *Allegations by the Eire government concerning mal-treatment of the Roman Catholic minority in Northern Ireland arising out of partition.* Public Record Office, London DO 35/893/xii, November 1938.
3. *Fermanagh Times* 13 July 1933, and Northern Ireland Parliamentary Debates (Hansard), House of Commons, Vol.16, Col. 618, 21 March 1943.

concluded that there was "a marked tendency for Protestants to dominate the upper occupational classes while Catholics are found predominantly in the lower classes, thus the majority of Catholic men are either in semi-skilled or unskilled work or unemployed while Protestants are most likely to be in skilled or non-manual work". The same author found that "although Catholic men are less than 21% of the economically active population of both religions and both sexes, they represent 44% of the unemployed".[4] Catholic women did not fare much better. Later investigations by the official Fair Employment Agency (FEA) in the '70s concluded that "there is no doubt that Engineering Crafts have not been equally open to all" and that "in two companies it was not disputed that the skilled fitters and similar tradesman ... almost certainly did not include a Catholic".[5] The FEA also concluded that "the numbers and proportions of Roman Catholics in the higher echelons of the Civil Service are very small".[6] This pattern was repeated at local government level where in 1968 out of 77 school bus drivers in County Fermanagh, which had a small Catholic majority, only three were Catholics.[7] All this meant a lot in an area which always had a much higher level of unemployment than in Britain.

Housing was another grievance. Unionist-controlled local councils failed to provide housing for needy Catholic families, especially in those areas where the councils had been gerrymandered to create artificial Unionist majorities. Voting was restricted to householders and housing too many Catholics would give them votes. Housing standards were bad anyway, and this policy led to a real housing crisis in areas like Derry City in the mid-'60s.

Overseeing this situation were the Special Powers Act and

4. E.A. Aunger, "Religion and Class: An analysis of 1971 Census Data", in R.J. Cormack and R.D. Osborne (eds), *Religion, Education and Employment, Aspects of Equal Opportunity in Northern Ireland.* Appletree Press 1983, pp 33 and 39.
5. Fair Employment Agency for Northern Ireland, *Report on Employment Patterns in the Belfast area with particular reference to engineering.* Belfast: FEA 1983, pp 7 and 10.
6. Fair Employment Agency for Northern Ireland, *Report of an investigation by the Fair Employment Agency for Northern Ireland into the non-industrial Northern Ireland Civil Service.* Belfast: FEA 1983, p 13.
7. Fermanagh Civil Rights Association, *Fermanagh Facts.* Enniskillen 1969, p 27.

the B Specials. The Special Powers Act, a permanent emergency law, gave the government power to ban organizations, meetings and publications, to seize property, to restrict the movements of individuals or exclude them from its territory, to suspend jury trial, to search or arrest without warrant and to imprison suspects without trial. All these powers were liberally used. The Irish Republican Army (IRA), Sinn Féin and other republican groups were banned together with their publications. Large numbers of militant nationalists were excluded from the state in the 1920s and hundreds of nationalists were interned without trial, many of them for years on end, in every decade of the state's existence. Militant nationalist activity, even by constitutional means, was illegal and the Act was also used occasionally to suppress militant workers. Meanwhile, in the background were the "Specials", an entirely Protestant and Unionist part-time and locally recruited militia that served like a private army for the Unionist Party and could be expanded and put on full-time duty at short notice. The heavily armed Specials, manning roadblocks in their own areas at night and stopping and questioning their Catholic neighbours, were a constant source of complaint by nationalists.

There were occasional spurts of activity by the underground IRA, the remnant of the force that had fought for independence in the '20s, but they were easily crushed by the ruthless use of internment without trial. There was a constitutional Nationalist Party with about a dozen MPs in the 52-member local parliament, but it was cautious, conservative, Catholic-church dominated and, above all, totally ineffective. Frustrated nationalists had periodically appealed to the Dublin government to come to their aid but had received little support. Meanwhile, the Unionist regime had done a deal with the Catholic church over religious schools when the state was set up, and so the church was quiet. A small Catholic professional class — doctors, lawyers etc. — served its own community and was by and large content. The rest of the Catholic/nationalist population was sullen and resentful, but cowed. Anger could flare up suddenly, as in October 1964 when armed police tore down an Irish flag in Sinn Féin's election headquarters in the Catholic Falls Road area of Belfast and sparked off three nights of bitter rioting, but for the most part the nationalist population was quiescent.

The hopes of nationalists were raised a little in the early '60s. A new Unionist leader, Captain Terence O'Neill, took over from Lord Brookeborough in 1963. He was less overtly sectarian than his predecessor and was anxious to project a better image abroad to help attract outside investment. He also wanted economic co-operation with the Dublin government. He made noises about better community relations within Northern Ireland and in January 1965 he met the Dublin Taoiseach, Sean Lemass — the first meeting between the Belfast and Dublin leaders since 1925. In Britain a Labour government was elected in 1964, after having spent 13 years out of office. Labour was traditionally sympathetic to Irish nationalism and nationalists in Northern Ireland hoped that Harold Wilson's government might use its ultimate control over Belfast to force the Unionists to bring in some reforms.

In 1964 a group of Catholic professionals established a Campaign for Social Justice to compile statistics about discrimination and lobby for reform. They worked closely with the British National Council for Civil Liberties and the Campaign for Democracy in Ulster, a pressure group within the British Labour Party. In 1966 Gerry Fitt, an opposition MP in the Stormont parliament, was elected to the British House of Commons for West Belfast, the first nationalist representative there for eleven years. Now the nationalists had a voice at Westminster and, they hoped, a sympathetic government which would listen to them. Reform seemed to be in the air. Local trade union leaders and even the mainly Protestant and strongly pro-Partition Northern Ireland Labour Party called for moves against discrimination — though the Labour Party call came only after pressure from students and Young Socialists.

But it soon became apparent that the lobbying approach and Terence O'Neill's honeyed words did not produce results. No reforms were made and Northern Ireland government decisions seemed to be based on the same old sectarian considerations. O'Neill's government decided that the region needed an alternative economic focus to Belfast, but instead of injecting capital and directing investment into the deprived and underdeveloped second city of Derry, which already had a port and an industrial base, the government decided to create a new city based on the inland market towns of Portadown and Lurgan in north County Armagh. The conclusion seemed obvious: Derry had a Catholic majority; north Armagh was staunchly and safely Protestant. Then the government decided to establish a second university in the North. Once again Derry was the obvious choice and it already had a small university college to act as a nucleus. But at the end of 1964 it was announced that the new university would be located in the small but solidly Unionist north coast town of Coleraine.

Then, in the mid-'60s, members of Sinn Féin, anxious to get involved in open political activity, set up Republican Clubs in an attempt to get round the ban on their organization, but in March 1967 Home Affairs Minister Bill Craig banned the Clubs under the Special Powers Act and threw in a ban on commemorations of the centenary of the Fenian Rising in 1867 for good measure. There were countless other minor decisions as well which seemed to reflect all the old bigotry. There was no sign of real change. On the contrary, there was a backlash in the Unionist movement against O'Neill's meetings with Lemass and his purely verbal moderation. The backlash was led by an ultra-loyalist fundamentalist preacher, Reverend Ian Paisley. It soon expressed itself in other forms as well when in 1966 a loyalist paramilitary group, calling itself after the pre-1922 Ulster Volunteer Force, killed three people in sectarian attacks in Belfast. O'Neill's government banned the revived UVF, but from then on they ran scared of the loyalist backlash and seemed to abandon any plans they had for reform. Meanwhile the nationalist population, its hopes raised and then dashed again, was growing impatient and Derry City was turning into a powder keg.

The setting up of the Republican Clubs had been part of a new departure in the republican movement — Sinn Féin and the IRA — following the collapse of a campaign of armed raids across the borders of Northern Ireland at the end of the '50s. Conscious of their political isolation and lack of mass support, the remnants of the movement decided to turn to open political and social agitation in both parts of Ireland. The new departure had been boosted by the commemorations in 1966 of the 50th anniversary of the 1916 Easter Rising which revived interest in the half-suppressed writings of James Connolly, the marxist trade union leader who had been one of the leaders of the Rising. Connolly's socialist vision and life of agitation were more attractive to a younger generation of republicans than narrow mystical nationalism and accorded better with the spirit of the times. In the North the republicans began to involve themselves in social agitation and became interested in co-operating with other groups to oppose repression and discrimination within the Northern state. Talks were held with the middle class Catholic reformers and a handful of Communist Party members, trade unionists and Protestant liberals, and in March 1967 all these strands and a

INSTITIÚID TEICNEOLAÍOCHTA
AN LEABHARLANN
LEITIR CEANAINN
323.
4094
5003353 7

couple of representatives of the student radicals at Queen's University — came together to set up the Northern Ireland Civil Rights Association (NICRA). It was seen at first as primarily a lobbying and propagandist organization, but events outside the North were having their effect on the people involved in setting up NICRA as well. Middle-aged and middle-class Catholic reformers were not overly concerned about the Vietnam war, Che Guevara, or student uprisings, but even they were affected by the black civil rights movement in the United States, seeing in it parallels with their own position. And the tactics of the American movement, its marches, pickets and sit-ins, appealed to the younger elements involved, especially in the republican movement.

In the summer of 1968, in protest at housing discrimination by Dungannon Council, a local Republican Club encouraged homeless Catholic families to squat in vacant council houses in the village of Caledon, County Tyrone. The families were evicted, one of them to make room for the single and childless secretary of a Unionist Party candidate. A local Nationalist MP, Austin Currie, briefly occupied the vacant house accompanied by television cameras, and NICRA was persuaded to back a march from the village of Coalisland to Dungannon a month later to protest at the council's discriminatory policies. It was Northern Ireland's first civil rights march.

I was among a couple of car loads of Young Socialists and students joined the march from Belfast where we had just held our own march earlier in the day in protest at the week-old Soviet invasion of Czechoslovakia. For us it was a symbolic fusing of the international student rebellion with the smouldering revolt against the specific grievances of Northern Ireland, but when we arrived in Coalisland we had an immediate clash with the stewards of the civil rights march, who objected to our red banner and the flag of the Vietnamese National Liberation Front, left over from our regular Saturday afternoon protests against the war in Vietnam. The alliance of student radicals and solid respectable nationalists taking reluctantly to the streets was not to be roses all the way. But when the march ended, blocked by the RUC from entering the town of Dungannon (which had a small nationalist majority), the stewards and the crowd joined in singing "We Shall Overcome", the anthem of the US civil rights movement. International events had influenced all of us.

All that summer the local Republican Club in Derry and a

group of young left-wingers in the local Labour Party had been squatting families and staging protests over the housing crisis in the city and the discriminatory policies of the Unionist city council. They asked NICRA to back a march in Derry at the beginning of October, which it did with some reluctance. The cautious middle class elements on the NICRA executive were getting worried: things were moving too fast for them. When Home Affairs Minister Bill Craig banned the march they wanted to call it off, but the local activists were determined to go ahead. The leading left-wing activist, Eamonn McCann, was a former student radical and shared a background of involvement in a small London-based Trotskyist organization, the Irish Workers Group, with some of us in the Young Socialists and student movement in Belfast. He had no difficulty in getting our support to defy the ban. Rank and file republicans were keen to go ahead as well, and NICRA was told the march would go ahead without them. In the end they agreed to come.

The rest is the stuff of this book. The police attack on the demonstrators in Derry, some of them Queen's University students, sparked an instant reaction at the university, which was just reopening. This was our Paris, our Prague. Thousands of students took to the streets in protest over the next few days and the protest body set up within a week of the 5 October Derry march reflected the influence of the Paris uprising. It was called Peoples Democracy and had mass open-ended discussions with no structures, no rules and supposedly no leaders. And it had the same sense of exhilaration, vitality and imagination that had characterised Paris that spring and must have marked Petrograd during the 1917 Russian revolution, Havana when Fidel Castro and Che Guevara entered it in 1959 and Managua when the Sandinistas triumphed in 1979. It had the same subversive effect as well, spreading out to wider and wider circles, to school students, to young workers, and calling in question not only the Stormont government but most other institutions in society as well.

The reaction of the general public, at least in the nationalist community, was only slightly slower than that of the students, and 15,000 people marched in Derry five weeks after 5 October. The minority population was in revolt. Peoples Democracy was only one strand in that revolt. The republican movement was the other major strand, and then the respectable Catholic middle class, always lagging behind and always the first to pull out when the going got rough or when they thought they had got enough for themselves. But Peoples Democracy and its precursor, the Young Socialists, was perhaps the group which best expressed the spirit of the worldwide youth revolt of 1968 within the civil rights movement in the North of Ireland. For that reason most of the contributors to this book are from that current, though that is not to underrate the contribution of the other currents, nor of those, especially in the republican movement and the left of the Labour movement, who fought against the oppression and injustice of the Northern state in previous generations and kept the spirit of resistance and the ideals of republicanism and socialism alive in darker times.

Bernadette McAliskey (Bernadette Devlin, as she was then) is the name most identified of all with Peoples Democracy. Here she reflects on a less well-known aspect of her career — her term in the British parliament as probably the only student revolutionary to win a parliamentary election in that period of upheaval. And she tells how she tried to strengthen the links between the struggle of the nationalist minority in the North of Ireland and black militants in the United States — to the consternation of her more respectable supporters. Since then she has continued to fight tirelessly against injustice and for the rights of prisoners in particular, despite narrowly escaping death in an assassination attempt in 1981.

Eilis McDermott, Inez McCormack and Ed Moloney were less well-known Peoples Democracy activists, although Eilis went to the United States to represent Peoples Democracy and met the Black Panthers even before Bernadette McAliskey did. They have followed different paths since those days. Eilis McDermott has become a lawyer, defending many of those accused in political cases in Northern Ireland's non-jury "Diplock" courts, notably in some of the major "supergrass" trials of the early '80s. She writes about the corruption of the law and the courts as tools of the British government's counter-insurgency strategy in the North.

Inez McCormack has become Northern Ireland's leading woman trade unionist, organizing and fighting on behalf of low-paid workers in the public service. She has also fought a long and often lonely battle against both religious and sex discrimination in the North, lending her name to the campaign for the MacBride Principles in the United States as a method of combatting the job discrimination which played such a major part in sparking off the whole civil rights campaign.

Ed Moloney became a journalist in the mid-'70s, working at first with the Belfast Workers Research Unit and the investigative journal *Hibernia*. He pioneered a type of probing journalism which tried to get behind the daily recital of violent incidents and regurgitation of official press releases to show the real roots of the problem in Northern Ireland. On the way he was responsible for exposing many of the murkier aspects of the security forces' dirty war in the North. He remains one of the best investigative journalists covering Northern Ireland affairs.

Margaret Ward was one of the school students subverted by Peoples Democracy and the events of October 1968, but her contribution is a timely reminder that for all our revolutionary fervour we were still products of our time, and the attitude of the male leadership of the movement on women's issues was not much better than that of the establishment we were fighting against. However, the upheaval of 1968 did help to bring forward a new generation of women activists, who questioned the whole basis of the social as well as political structures around them and created a new women's movement in the North of Ireland. She tells of her part in that story.

Geoffrey Bell was not a member of Peoples Democracy but he was a student in Derry in the years before 5 October 1968, influenced both by international events and by what was happening around him in the streets. He was active in the Labour Party group there around Eamonn McCann and went on to become prominent in Irish solidarity organizations in Britain and to write about the political history of Ulster Protestants and the British Labour Party's record on Ireland. He is now a leading figure in the Labour Committee on Ireland.

Carol Coulter was a leading activist in the Young Socialists in Dublin, with whom the Belfast Young Socialists and later Peoples Democracy had close contacts. Her article reminds us that the events of the late '60s also had their impact in the South of Ireland, and especially in Dublin, where the appalling housing conditions had generated their own struggle led by the Dublin Housing Action Committee. She details some of those developments as well as tracing the repercussions of events in the North on the Southern scene.

Gerry Adams comes from that other major strand in the civil rights campaign, the republican movement. As a young republican he was part of the shift to the left and towards involvement in political agitation that marked the republican movement in the late '60s following the reassessment of the '50s Border campaign. I remember meeting him in the period he writes about, before 1968, to discuss the campaign against slum housing in West Belfast in which he was involved. He was accompanied by Joe McCann, a charismatic left-wing republican who was gunned down by British paratroops in 1972. Gerry Adams writes of his personal perception of the developments in the republican movement as the civil rights movement began to get off the ground. His perspective is the more interesting because he was one of the relatively few republicans involved in the new departure who did not follow the road that later led to the Workers' Party. He has, of course, progressed since then to become president of Sinn Féin and MP for West Belfast.

The contributors are a mixed group. Several of them come from a Protestant background and a majority are women so they are not statistically representative of the civil rights movement, but they do indicate something of its diversity and non-sectarian nature, and something of the extent to which women involved in the movement have played a more prominent role in subsequent years. They do not all share the same views on the current situation in Northern Ireland or on the way forward, but their accounts serve to capture some of the spirit and atmosphere of that crucial and remarkable period in 1968-69 and to indicate how some of the activists of that period see things now. Perhaps there may be enough common ground in what they say to sketch out some of the steps needed to resolve the crisis that began 20 years ago with a popular revolt against the injustices of the sectarian state in Northern Ireland.

FACELESS MEN:
CIVIL RIGHTS AND AFTER

Inez McCormack was a student at Magee University College in Derry in the early 1960s when the Stormont government rejected it as the site for a second university in Northern Ireland. She was involved in the protests over that decision and then studied at Trinity College, Dublin. She was actively involved in Peoples Democracy in Belfast in 1968-69 and in solidarity work in London for the civil rights movement in 1970. She worked as a social worker in West Belfast from 1970 to '75 and was associated with the left-wing Newtownabbey Labour Party. She became a full-time official with the National Union of Public Employees in 1975 and NUPE regional organizer in 1980. In that year she also became the first woman from the North to be elected to the executive of the Irish Congress of Trade Unions, of which she is still a member. She is a member of the North's Equal Opportunities Commission and was a member of the board of the Fair Employment Agency, resigning in 1981 in protest at its ineffectiveness. She is one of the sponsors of the MacBride Principles for fair employment in Northern Ireland formulated in the United States.

People of my generation are all supposed to know precisely where they were on 22 November 1963, the day of John Kennedy's death. Knowing where you were on 5 October 1968, similarly marks you as a member of the civil rights generation in Northern Ireland. The place to be on that day was Duke Street in Derry, among the raggle-taggle group of middle-aged men in suits and young people with the fashionable lack of concern with personal appearance that identified them as anarchists, communists, or a variety of brands of socialist. This unlikely group had come together under the banner of civil rights, the banner of a movement which would shake the foundations of the Northern Ireland state.

I was not among that small group when the batons began to fly. On that day I was on a beach in Portugal, and learned of the march and the violent response to it next day, when local papers published a fuzzy photograph of baton-wielding policemen under the headline: "Religious riots in Ireland". Portugal was at that time still an "ideologically unsound" place to be. It was the last days of the fascist dictatorship, and CIA surgeons were said to be desperately trying to record electrical impulses from the brain stem of the otherwise dead dictator Salazar. We had hitched through the Continent to Portugal and something was haunting Europe that year. On the outskirts of Paris schoolkids a few years younger than ourselves put us up and regaled us with stories of their confrontations with the CRS, the riot police they had faced that May in Paris. We saw paramilitary police with their trucks and riot gear in the back streets of Rome making ready to attack demonstrating students and workers. And in London young people were also on the march, with the even-handed slogan of the New Left: "American troops out of Vietnam; Russian troops out of Czechoslovakia". Very few of those international demonstrators would have been aware of the problems of Ireland at the time; very few of them are not aware now. In particular, little did those youthful demonstrators in London know that in just over a year their own troops would be on the streets of Belfast, and would still be there when the Americans had long gone from Vietnam, and the demonstrators themselves had gone from youth to middle age.

That same year saw the assassination of a second Kennedy, and also of Martin Luther King. The latter in particular was to provide moral and practical inspiration for our own campaign. His voice still brings a prickle to the back of my neck, and more than any other brings back the events of the early civil rights days and their atmosphere of determined, good-humoured optimism. His voice also has a peculiar resonance for me and my subsequent career for two reasons. Firstly, it is in his campaigns that you first begin to see the emergence of a powerful and dangerous force — women; black women courteously declining to give up their seats in buses and restaurants and accepting the violent abuse with what looks like resignation but is not. And secondly King had gone to Memphis, where he was killed, to organize black garbage collectors in order to deepen his challenge to an increasingly frightened state. His inspiration derived from his capacity to identify a mass constituency of the wretched; to point out to them that their wretchedness did not inhere in their persons; to identify its source in an uncaring and racist state; and persuade them of their capacity to change their condition through collective action.

5 October 1968 was an important date, and not just for symbolic reasons. Real blood resulted from the violent reaction of the RUC to the civil rights march that day in Derry and the anger rippled far beyond Derry's city boundaries. It was, therefore, a turning point. But there are many dates that might qualify as the starting point for the civil rights campaign, and it is foolish to try to date specifically the powerful social phenomenon that the civil rights movement became. While I did not take part in the 5 October march, I had been involved four years earlier in an event which might have set alarm bells ringing in the Unionist establishment had it not been for their blinding belief in their capacity to maintain their supremacy with the help of a raft of repressive laws and their stranglehold on democracy. This was the "University for Derry" campaign.

Although my own background was Protestant, I count myself fortunate to have lived in Derry while I attended Magee University College, and subsequently I lived and studied in Dublin, thereby encountering Catholic culture with its infuriating and perplexing mixture of political radicalism and social conservatism. In 1964, while I was studying at Magee, the Lockwood Report recommended the siting of a new university for Northern Ireland at Coleraine, bypassing Derry with its nucleus of a campus in a blatantly political decision that united the city in outrage. The focus of the rage was what became known as the "Seven Faceless Men" — leading Unionist citizens who became latter-day Lundys by pleading the cause of Coleraine over that of their own city for sectarian purposes. Popular feeling led to direct action of a modest sort in the organization of a "motorcade" to Stormont for the debate on the Lockwood Report. The debate was marked by a ferocious attack on the Unionist government by the maverick Unionist MP, Desmond Boal. While the demand for recognition for Derry in this and many other areas failed, it taught the people a lesson in organization which was to stand them in good stead a few years later when "the Capital City of Injustice" rose in peaceful and determined revolt against the state which had attempted so often to humiliate them. It taught me a lesson, too: that often democratic decisions are overturned and legitimate rights denied by faceless men, who publicly espouse democracy but practise squalid self-seeking deals and engage in influence-mongering behind closed doors. Like the "Seven Faceless Men" of Derry, they are often those who assure you publicly of their support. Another lesson taught by this episode was that the same politically-motivated decisions are now repeated by British Direct Rule Ministers with the same arrogance as the Unionists of old. Part of the argument of the "University for Derry" campaign was that a campus at Coleraine would not prosper, and so it proved. Yet when 20 years after the original decision it was clear that the new university had failed, British Direct Rule Ministers yielded to political pressure and reprieved it in a merger with the Northern Ireland Polytechnic. These same Ministers have no qualms about closing hospitals and schools.

On our return from Portugal in mid-October of 1968, we found the political situation utterly transformed. Students in Belfast had established a semi-permanent sit-in at the city centre and Queen's University was turned into a revolutionary centre with its own equivalent of the French student leader, Danny the Red — only this time it was a woman, Bernadette Devlin. However, nowhere was the transformation more evident than in Derry. After 5 October the Minister for Home Affairs announced a blanket ban on marches in the city, thereby unwittingly providing endless opportunities for the citizenry to demonstrate that the law was an ass. A stroll to the sweetie shop with a mate was declared a march, and the might of the state thereby defied. Pubs on the west bank of the river Foyle seemed to have given up their primary job of selling drink and were transformed into licensed political clubs where Lenin, Trotsky and Connolly were discussed in detail hitherto reserved for the performance of footballers and greyhounds. Of course, it is easy to fall into the trap of uncritically romanticising those days, and it is not my job to analyse them in any detail, though I can scarcely resist the temptation to give some snapshot memories: of Fergus Woods, the Peoples Democracy candidate in Newry in the 1969 Stormont election, his alarm when it looked as if he might be elected, and his relief when a recount resulted in his defeat — not because he or any of us were afraid of power but because Stormont represented to us the corruption of power, and in any case we already regarded it as a corpse; of taking 24 hours out of that election campaign to get married in a church in East Belfast on what was subsequently to become International Women's Day, having been turned down by two Catholic churches beforehand, mixed marriages being still frowned on; of being the target of petrol bombs at the end of the march to Derry; of the remark of a young Unionist after that march when police went on the rampage in the Bogside assaulting women — "Who would want to rape those women anyway?"

Although there was an undoubted element of elitism, particularly in the student movement, I do recall the busloads of factory workers who came to meet the march to Derry at Burntollet bridge on the outskirts of the city. It was for them we were fighting, and we were giving voice to the voiceless. Many of them are now well able to speak for themselves.

I think part of the reason for our success was our naïvety and innocence, and my own politicisation was slow, irregular and halting. I was a member of Newtownabbey Labour Party, whose non-sectarian tolerance and radicalism threatened to give the Northern Ireland Labour Party a good name. It was their acceptance of eccentrics which gave me confidence in my own ability, and as the heady '60s gave way to the grim '70s members of that party like Bob Kidd, Roger and Deirdre Byrne and Tommy Davidson worked ceaselessly and thanklessly at combatting sectarian violence in the estates of Newtownabbey. They were prepared to do the donkey work for the emerging "community relations" industry without being absorbed into what was to become a self-regarding and ineffectual body.

In 1970 I was appointed, with two close friends, to social work positions by Belfast Corporation. We were all three Protestant, and all three were appointed to West Belfast. Our suspicion that we were not expected to rock the boat was soon confirmed by the lack of support and resources we got. The time

I spent there radicalised me in a way nothing else could. There was a war going on there, and not just the war between the emerging Provisionals and the British army but a war to survive under Third World conditions and to preserve some vestige of self-respect in the face of universal contempt. The social services office in which we worked was a cosmetic exercise which did not even deserve the Victorian label of welfare, which at least provided some relief. Our job was to perceive and treat these people as victims of their own inadequacy, as hopeless cases. In those five years, against a backdrop of violence, our problems came not from our clients but from the insensitivity and lack of concern of the social services bureaucracy. Not only was it the case that the gains of the civil rights movement had made no difference to the lives of the mass of the people there, but the state had the power even to remove what little rights they had. Thus the introduction of the Payment for Debt Act in 1971, ostensibly to break the rent and rates strike which followed the introduction of internment without trial, allowed the state to withdraw every single penny to which these people were entitled. When I complained that this was hitting women very severely I was told (by another faceless man) that I could advise them "to withdraw their conjugal rights from their husbands". When we began to agitate for minimal resources we were victimised by the social services bureaucracy who threatened to close the office, using the Troubles as an excuse. It was at this stage that we joined the National Union of Public Employees (NUPE) to protect ourselves. I knew its local secretary, the late John Coulthard, through the Northern Ireland Labour Party and also because of his work on welfare benefits cases. John was a decent and honourable man who had fallen among thieves. He had come from England to be manager of Northern Ireland Railways, but left after trying to introduce parity of pay with Britain. His honesty and commitment made him few friends in the trade union movement.

I began working part-time for NUPE and was appointed a full-time organizer in 1975. Its General Secretary, Alan Fisher, who like John also died this year (1988), was also prepared to trust me, and I was fortunate to have those two men who did not feel threatened by women as bosses. We organized those at what were regarded as the lowest levels of the public sector who had by and large been ignored by the trade union movement. Their marginality made them easy prey for the faceless men who employed them, and they often came from areas like those I had worked in as a social worker. They were mainly women, whose very low pay was the only household income in areas of mass unemployment. One of the first groups I recruited were home helps, who in the early '70s earned as little as five shillings (25p) an hour, and each marginal and bitterly won improvement in their pay and conditions was met on the part of their employers by cuts in their hours so that they were little better off. In later years our members in the public services would be involved in a series of bruising and often "unpopular" disputes. They have acted in the knowledge that struggle would involve personal vilification and victimisation, that the odds were stacked against them, and that in the unlikely event of victory they would have to fight again in order to ensure that it was not snatched from them. Their good-humoured determination and imagination in struggle is the closest I have come to the enthusiasm of the early civil rights movement.

Women trade union officials were rare in 1975, and still are, but it was useful to have the odd token woman in a position of prominence. In 1980 with John Coulthard's encouragement I stood for and was elected to the executive of the Irish Congress of Trade Unions. I can think of no other trade unionist who would have permitted a junior officer (and a woman!) to stand in his place. The atmosphere and ethos of the trade union movement was, like that of the civil rights movement, male and patronising. I recall that when I was first elected to the executive I remarked that in the trade union movement, like any other male preserve, a woman was a "grand wee girl" provided she confined her activities to the equivalent of making tea and sandwiches; once she demonstrated she had a mouth in her head and a thought in her brain, she became "that bitch". And so it proved. It took three years to persuade the movement to agree to the modest reform of reserved seats on the executive for women, and bringing the proposal forward brought charges from the nominal left of introducing discrimination and division. They are charges I have learned to live with in a variety of areas. The perceived motivation of status and position is now acceptable. The wish to exercise power for and by women who have neither is still regarded as disloyal and divisive. The myriad demands of women ranging from individual health to equal pay, through to community action, can no longer be ghettoised as "women's issues". They set the agenda of the future and the movements relevance in this and the next century will depend on its response to these demands in practice rather than rhetoric.

In 1976 I was appointed trade union nominee to the Northern Ireland Equal Opportunities Commission (EOC) and the Fair Employment Agency (FEA), charged respectively with dealing with sex and religious discrimination. I am well aware of the limitations of legislation in changing people's lives and securing their rights. Unlike the present Secretary of State for Northern Ireland, Tom King, I saw the outlawing of discrimination as a beginning rather than an end. Laws banning denials of basic rights are useless without adequate enforcement, and my civil rights and trade union experience taught me that there was no shortage of faceless men ready to dilute and pervert the law. In any case the issue of discrimination on any grounds is too important, and legislation against it is too hard won not to use, defend and extend the protection it affords. Initially the Direct Rule administration resisted attempts to extend the Sex Discrimination Act to Northern Ireland, and it required a campaign on the part of the emerging women's movement to persuade them to do so. Ms Jo Richardson, the Labour MP, was of crucial importance in the success of the campaign. As I suspected, right from the very beginning of the work of both the EOC and the FEA attempts were made to weaken their impact. The EOC had a part-time "chairman" (the commission itself insisted upon the sexist designation) and went about its task with a part-time commitment. The attitude to enforcement was slovenly, and there was little attempt made to address seriously the lack of rights of women. One day two very junior members of the staff of the commission knocked on my door. They were young, inexperienced and angry. They had complained about serious irregularities in the processing of cases but had been ignored, and they asked my advice on how they should proceed. I told them they could withdraw their complaints and apologise, or they could pursue them with my support and be prepared to lose their jobs. They chose the latter course without hesitation.

With their help, and in the teeth of furious opposition, I managed to get agreement to an independent investigation of the commission. This was highly critical, especially in the area of enforcement, and recommended a root and branch restructuring of the commission, which effectively meant starting off from scratch. But there was extreme resistance to implementation of the proposals, from the Labour Secretary of State Don Concannon down. I and the other trade union nominee on the commission were withdrawn in order to force the Secretary of State's hand, and we were helped by the publicising of the issue in The Irish Times by David McKittrick and Fionnuala O'Connor. Eventually the proposals were implemented by the incoming Conservative Minister of State, Mr Rossi, partly because of the unsavoury publicity, and partly because rumblings were beginning to force a similar investigation into the efficiency of the Fair Employment Agency. The upshot was the appointment of a full-time chair and legal enforcement officer to the EOC.

Since that time the commission has, within its limits, pursued the rights of women in Northern Ireland with considerable vigour, placing the British commission in the shade. A commission which manages to get RUC chief Sir Jack Hermon into the witness box, and takes on the RUC in court and wins, can take some pride in the achievement. This was a sex discrimination case taken by a number of RUC women reservists and settled in their favour. The real importance of the work of the commission is that by being prepared to service and fight for the rights of women in such areas as sexual harassment and equal value it has encouraged women's confidence to speak for themselves and to fight for their own rights.

Job discrimination was a principal factor giving rise to the civil rights agitation, and it was only as a result of such action that the British government moved to address the situation. The government set up the Cameron Commission to investigate the causes of the unrest. Its report documented with a cold authority how discrimination was embedded administratively, socially, politically and economically into the organization of life in the province. The agitation for equal rights continued with death on the streets here and a bad press abroad. Stung by the latter, the British government then set up the Van Straubenzee Working Party on discrimination in employment, which reported in 1974 and, like the Cameron Report, still bears reading. However, only some of its recommendations were embodied in the Fair Employment Act of 1976, and the thrust of the legislation did not match that of the Report. The Fair Employment Agency which was set up to "enforce" the Act began its work in 1976. With its arrival, the sharp focus of the Cameron Report was blurred. By taking as its main purpose the need not to offend anybody and by its supine willingness to give priority to the demands of the government over the needs of those the law charged it with protecting, the agency ended up offending nearly everyone, except, of course, the government. Employers more or less ignored it, public bodies ran rings around it. After four years an independent review of the agency concluded: "The experience of the legal enforcement of the Fair Employment Act, thus far, is a depressing picture of a massive task, of the possibility of change, but of an agency which has failed to meet that challenge."

In spite of this, the British government tactic of substituting image for reality worked for half a dozen years. From 1976 to 1982 the issue of discrimination was removed from the agenda. On the rare occasions when it was brought up, the government merely pointed out that the Fair Employment Act had made discrimination illegal, and the agency was dealing with "residual problems". Indeed, with the practised arrogance of the Unionist bigot, vintage early '60s, the government played down the historical significance of the issue. Thus the British Information Service in Washington said: "While we don't deny discrimination may have existed it *was,*" [and I emphasise the was] "probably not to the extent often alleged." The government might by now have been in a position to run down the FEA and declare the problem solved, to the applause of the international community, had the acid reality not corroded the carefully constructed image. The government's own statistics began to show from the early '80s that not only had the reality of discrimination not changed since the '60s, it had actually worsened. Another factor threatened further loss of government control over the issue — the external factor. Those of us who sought to use the internal mechanisms to achieve real change, and had received nothing but unveiled contempt for our pains, welcomed the growing US interest in the issue of employment equality.

In the meantime there was a long struggle to raise the question of employment equality within the trade union movement. The history and development of this issue has reflected both the division of the communities in Northern Ireland, and the strength of union organization amongst skilled craft workers. However, the balance and structure of the movement has changed with the growth of service industries and the recruitment of Catholics in unskilled and clerical grades. In the name of trade union unity attempts to raise and face the issues of division were regarded as at best utopian and at worst sectarian and divisive. That reaction was common both from those to whom it provided a respectable defence of an indefensible status quo and those who genuinely believed that it was impossible to tackle the issue without "dividing the shop floor". As a woman, however, I had long since learned that to beg the question of inequality is to accept injustice as the price of unity. I had also learned that such unity was in reality defined as the needs of the dominant self interest. The official view of the movement has been to support the principles of fair employment and the Fair Employment Agency, but to avoid involvement in the issue of changing work practices. That view is beginning to change.

I take some pride in the fact that my union, though small and made up of low-paid Catholic and Protestant workers, has since the mid-'70s consistently argued the case for affirmative action programmes in employment. That was not a popular view with the British government when we first raised it, and I imagine it is no more so now. It was not a popular view within the trade union movement either, but support for this position has grown. The change can be shown by the fact that in 1981 a motion to the ICTU Northern Ireland Committee Conference from my union to attach affirmative action conditions to the investment of public funds only received the support of our own delegation. At a similar conference less than five years later, a similar motion from my union was passed unanimously. External pressure has forced the issue to the top of the agenda and continuing arguments against the possibility of change are revealed as defence mechanisms.

I am well aware that unemployed Catholics in West Belfast are unlikely to be impressed with resolutions at trade union conferences. We have done no more than identify and name the problem. But even that took years of often bitter controversy within a movement which prides itself on being progressive. In any case, the effectiveness of the trade union movement is limited. It has little responsibility for control of employment and, by the nature of Irish politics, it is marginalised. I therefore welcomed support from the international solidarity of labour in the fight to create genuine and positive change.

The Sean MacBride Principles, a set of equal opportunity principles for Northern Ireland, were formulated because the British government refused to budge in response to internal pressure, and because, far from the problem having been resolved, discrimination had actually worsened in the ten years of the FEA's operation. The Principles were launched in the States by the Irish National Caucus. The first signatory was the late Sean MacBride, Ireland's most distinguished jurist. Some people have a problem with the name, since he was chief-of-staff of the IRA — in the '30s. Against this his Nobel and Lenin Peace Prizes, his renunciation of violence, and his belief in a constitutional republican solution apparently count as nothing. The two remaining signatories both come from Protestant backgrounds: John Robb, a surgeon who, while living and working in Northern Ireland, sits in the Dublin Senate; and myself. I thought long and hard before signing, and only did so after assurances from fellow trade unionists in the States that the Principles had the support of the AFL - CIO. I should also make it clear that my position is a personal one.

One of the features of the British government's campaign against the Principles is to call into question the motives of those who support them. This has two advantages for the authorities: they don't have to address the issue and can engage in mudslinging and guilt by association. The three signatories mentioned had many political differences. We signed the Principles because we agreed with their content, and considered them an absolute necessity, having despaired of finding an "internal" solution. The Principles themselves were modelled closely on the Sullivan Principles directed against apartheid in South Africa. While none of the signatories of the MacBride Principles has sought to make anything of this connection, it has, however, particularly incensed the British government, who themselves constantly bring it up. If people want to cut a stick to beat themselves, it's very difficult to stop them...

The essential difference between the Principles and anything which the government has proposed is simply this: the former address the reality of discrimination in Northern Ireland; call for contract compliance; for measures to ensure that Catholics are appropriately represented in apprentice schemes, so they can gain appropriate qualifications in order to compete for jobs on their own merits; and for reasonable measures to protect them going to and from work. It is these elements of the Principles that have called down the wrath of Mr King and his civil servants. "Bussing! Quotas! Reverse discrimination!" they splutter, while they for their part ignore their responsibility and prepare yet another glossy PR job to protect their own image.

The Principles have been a barnstorming success in the States, penetrating well beyond the Irish-American community and gaining ground much more rapidly than the Sullivan Principles. They were first signed into law in Massachusetts by Governor

Michael Dukakis in 1985. At that time he was virtually unknown outside his own state. As I write he is the Democratic nominee for President and looks likely to win the election. He has promised to make the MacBride Principles American law if elected. Already eight states have adopted the Principles and another half-dozen are likely to do so in the near future. The reasons for the success of the MacBride campaign are not too difficult to fathom. First, Irish-Americans 20 years ago were in a position similar to Northern Ireland Protestants now. They had a deplorable record on civil rights and were forced, as one put it to me, to "clean up their act". They realise this will be as painful for Northern Protestants as it was for them, but they also realise there is no other way ahead. Indeed, some of those who are particularly intimately involved with the MacBride campaign in the Irish-American Labour Coalition (an AFL - CIO affiliate) were also involved in the implementation of civil rights legislation in Boston, an experience which they have described to me as painful, but valuable and necessary. Secondly, MacBride has offered an ethical, legal and moderate avenue to effect real change in the lives of working people in Northern Ireland; hence the rich diversity of the campaign for MacBride in the States, embracing the mainstream of religious, political and trade union groups.

The response of the British government has been to repeat the errors of the past in a quite astonishing way. The Standing Advisory Commission on Human Rights in Northern Ireland (SACHR) published a damning analysis of the ineffectiveness of the Fair Employment Act in 1987. More than a decade after discrimination in employment had been outlawed, Catholic males were two and a half times more likely to be unemployed than their Protestant counterparts, and females fared little better. Like the Van Straubenzee Report, SACHR spelt out a detailed framework for effective change. In May 1988 the British government's White Paper outlining a new Fair Employment Act was published with legislation to follow late in 1988. It ignored many crucial elements of SACHR's recommendations, and only grudgingly admitted the reality of discrimination. But this time I do not believe that the British government will get away with further ploys as easily as they did in 1976 after the introduction of the Fair Employment Act. To begin with their evasion of the issue to date has been too transparent, while the MacBride principles now act as an effective counter to British manoeuvring.

I believe that I can best sum up my own activities and beliefs by quoting from the evidence I gave to the Massachusetts State Legislature, before Governor Michael Dukakis became the first American statesman to sign the MacBride Principles into legislation.

"I have seen it as my responsibility both because of my background and my present responsibilities as a leader of a union which represents both Catholics and Protestants; as a leader of a movement which has historically represented Protestant advantage and Catholic disadvantage, to articulate what I see as the only road to the real unity of labour and of the movement and people to whom I belong. It is to face the issue of division, honestly and firmly in the open and to argue that divisions can only be bridged not by rhetoric or good will, but by the reality of change in behaviour. The responsibility for that change lies primarily with those who hold power and advantage. Change does not come easy at any time; it does not come easy in the midst of a war, it does not come easy for a women, it does not come easy for Protestant or Catholic. My Protestant members have thought about these things. It has not been comfortable for them, but if they can think about them then the Secretary of State for Northern Ireland can think about them.

"To oppose affirmative principles, which require effective practices, is to deny responsibility for change. I call into question the reality of any commitment to action based on words rather than deeds. It ultimately comes down to this. We can all deliver the rhetoric which offends nobody but the dispossessed. For those who have can always argue that tomorrow is the right time for change. For the have nots, today is not soon enough, and we can only hope for their generosity of spirit in forgetting their yesterdays."

A REPUBLICAN IN THE CIVIL RIGHTS CAMPAIGN

Gerry Adams was born in Belfast in 1948. He was educated at St Finian's primary school, St Gabriel's Intermediate School and St Mary's Grammar School, all in Belfast. He worked as a barman in the late 1960s and was active in the Republican Clubs and in the West Belfast Housing Action Committee. He was interned without trial from March to June 1972, when he was released and took part in discussions in London between republican representatives and the British government. He was interned again in July 1973 and later sentenced to four and a half years for attempting to escape. He was released in February 1976.

He spent seven months in jail in 1978 awaiting trial on a charge of IRA membership which was eventually dismissed. He became vice president of Sinn Féin in 1978. He was elected to the Northern Assembly in October 1982 and elected MP for West Belfast in June 1983. He was elected president of Sinn Féin later in 1983. He was wounded in an assassination attempt by the UDA in 1984. In 1987 he was re-elected MP for West Belfast.

The Ark wasn't a big public house. Situated at the corner of Broadbent Street on Belfast's Old Lodge Road, it consisted of a public bar, which was partitioned from the more discreet back room and snug. That was it. A backdrop of shelved whiskey bottles fronted by a no-nonsense wooden counter which separated myself and the only other barman from the clientele. He and I were Catholics. The customers were mostly Protestant, mainly male, and totally working class.

Porter was the staple and non-sectarian drink. Firkins of it were delivered weekly from Guinness's yard on the Grosvenor Road, manhandled into place behind the counter and dispensed with much care into pint glasses. No Double X or draught beers. Wee Willie Darks, bottles of Red Heart or Carling Black Label were minority brews. Either a wee Mundies or the cheaper Drawbridge wine offered a more popular deoch (drink). A bottle and a half 'un were strictly Friday or Saturday night treats. Sales of spirits were minimal. An occasional gin for the women to augment their more economical small sherries or port. No vodkas. No liqueurs. And no Pope.

All the customers lived beside the Ark or in neighbouring streets. These streets lay between the Old Lodge Road and the Shankill Road on one side and the Crumlin Road on the other. It was a loyalist area. The shipyard was the main source of employment and many of the Ark's male customers worked there. Or at least, as they put it themselves, they clocked in there most mornings. The majority of them were unskilled or semi-skilled labourers. More lucrative jobs were the preserve of better-off areas. Some of the customers were unemployed. They spent their time commuting between their homes, the bookies shop and the Ark. A few of them kept pigeons, some bred greyhounds. Rinty Monaghan, the former boxing champion, was the only celebrity to frequent the area.

The Twelfth of July provided an annual relief from the customary calmness. St Patrick's night in the Ark provided more entertainment. "When Irish Eyes are Smiling" and "The Green Glens of Antrim" vied with "The Boys of the County Armagh" and "Danny Boy" — minus the third verse of course. On one occasion I was moved to render a verse of "The Sash" in Irish. A Somme veteran followed me with a rendition of "Kevin Barry". At the end of the night as we cleared away glasses and empty bottles, everyone else stood for a collective voicing of "God Save the Queen". The Twelfth was a holiday. Not for bartenders of course, but for almost everyone else. Most of the Ark's clientele didn't go to the Field (where the annual Orange demonstration was held). Many of the men weren't in the Orange Order and none of the women were: they weren't allowed. We all watched the big parade of course and they crowded around the bonfires on the Eleventh night. They enjoyed themselves. There was no real harm in them. It was 1965. They felt under no threat and they presented no threat. That would come in its own time. They and we have only their leaders to thank for that.

In those pre-civil rights days I journeyed daily along the Falls Road, across the Shankill, and up the Old Lodge. Frequently I collected tripe, to be boiled with onions for a darts match buffet, from a Shankill Road butcher — no associate of his more notorious namesakes in later years (the "Shankill Butchers" were a loyalist murder gang) — and occasionally I took to the waters in Peter's Hill public baths at the bottom of the Shankill Road. On warm summer nights, including one Eleventh (of July) night, I walked to Ballymurphy along the Shankill and the West Circular Road, through miles of loyalist territory, stopping for a fish supper in the Eagle Supper Saloon on the way. Nobody bothered me. Maybe I didn't look like a Catholic. Or maybe nobody cared. Polarisation was peaceful. My only aggravation had occurred much earlier when a short-lived schoolboy boxing career came to an end in a Shankill Road club when a Malvern Street sparring partner took me and his pugilistic skills more seriously than I did. That was in 1958. I was ten.

When I worked in the Ark I was already involved in republican politics. When the planners started the destruction of the Falls Road with the demolition of the Loney area — a district of densely-packed tiny houses at the bottom of the Falls — and the building of the new slum of Divis Flats, I and other republicans joined local people in protest. When the same vandalism started in the Old Lodge Road I stood with locals at the door of the Ark and watched as the bulldozers destroyed and displaced a community. No one protested. Everyone was sad. Some of the women showed a little anger, but none of the local men listened to them: they were only women after all. And no one listened to me; I was only a wee Catholic barman.

Outside the Old Lodge Road, however, the snail's pace of progressive politics was slowly taking on a new momentum. In May 1965 a hesitant exchange of ideas between republicans, communists and unaffiliated trade unionists led to a conference on civil liberties hosted by the Belfast Trades Council. As well as the above individuals it was attended by the Northern Ireland Labour Party (NILP) and the Campaign for Social Justice. I was on the perimeter of such developments. Like the customers in the Ark, I was only subconsciously affected by them. Although the NILP temporarily thwarted the fragile unity which was emerging among the elements who attended the conference, the republicans, encouraged perhaps by these developments, were slowly coming out of the closet to challenge the Stormont government's Special Powers Act and the banning of Sinn Féin. Easter 1966 was marked by a large republican commemoration in West Belfast, while a month earlier someone blew up Nelson's Pillar in Dublin. And Ian Paisley initiated a new quarter century of long hot summers by leading a highly provocative and sectarian march into the nationalist Markets area of Belfast.

For my sins, in a hilarious Keystone Cops diversion, I was arrested for selling the republican paper, the *United Irishman*, as part of a Sinn Féin plan to flout a Stormont government ban on it. But meanwhile, more serious incidents, including the murders of two Catholics and a 70-year-old Protestant woman by the revived Ulster Volunteer Force led to the banning of the UVF by the Stormont government in 1966. Unionist boss Terence O'Neill had met Dublin Premier Sean Lemass the previous year, demonstrating that at least a section of Unionism was being reluctantly dragged into the twentieth century on the eve of the new EEC era.

By now I was working in another pub, the Duke of York in the centre of Belfast. I left the Ark following a wage dispute. I had asked for the union rate for working a public holiday — the Twelfth. Instead I got the sack; my own personal lock-out. I was sorry to leave my friends on the Old Lodge Road, and they, diminished in numbers by the on-going levelling of their homes, were sorry to see me go. Though I never thought of it then, I probably got sacked at a good time. Peaceful polarisation was fraying at the edges. Ironically it was my Catholic employer and not the Protestant customers who evicted me.

I was spending my long lunch breaks from the Duke of York churning out leaflets in Sinn Féin headquarters in Cyprus Street on a geriatric duplicating machine and learning the ground rules of political agitation. The Wolfe Tone Society, a republican-oriented discussion group, had re-invigorated the initiative which had led to the 1965 civil liberties conference. Another conference was held in Belfast in January 1967. It decided to start the Northern Ireland Civil Rights Association (NICRA). At the same time, and while involved in the preparation of this hesitant groundwork for a civil rights campaign, the republicans had embarked on their own initiative to transform the banned Sinn Féin party into an open, legal organization. Republican Clubs were formed for this purpose. They were banned as well.

In defiance of the ban, an open meeting of Republican Clubs was held in a room above a cafe in Belfast's Chapel Lane. We were pleasantly disappointed not to be arrested. A month later a meeting in the city's International Hotel elected an executive for the Northern Ireland Civil Rights Association and agreed on a constitution. We republicans were there in strength. We were acting on instructions not to pack the executive; it was sufficient to have an influence. We were also instructed to vote for Communist Party nominees. The meeting was uneventful with only the presence of a Unionist, Robin Cole, providing diversion for the younger republicans. Most of us had never seen a Unionist before, but he didn't look any different from anyone else. It was all a bit boring and I, for one, had no clear view of what it would come to mean.

For all that, it was an historic meeting. Over 20 years later at a conference in Coalisland to launch a '68 Committee, veteran republican Kevin Agnew gave me a hand-written list of those elected to that first executive. They were Dr Con McCloskey of the Campaign for Social Justice, Professor T. A. O'Brien, Noel Harris and Ken Banks of the draughtsman's union DATA, Professor Michael Dolley, Fred Heatley, Jack Bennet, Derek Peters of the Communist Party, Kevin Agnew, J. Quinn of the Liberal Party, Betty Sinclair of the Trades Council and Communist Party, Robin Cole, Joe Sherry of Gerry Fitt's Republican Labour Party and Paddy Devlin of the NILP. A backward glance over this first NICRA leadership shows how the republican voting strategy assured a nicely rounded leadership for the parent Civil Rights Association. Business concluded, everyone, voters and voted, went home. Few of us, including me, or, I guess, the newly elected executive, realised we had set in train the beginning of the end of 6 county politics as Unionism and the rest of us knew it. After years of sterling and patient preparatory work by a small number of committed progressives, a new era had yawned itself awake in the International Hotel at the back of Belfast's City Hall.

A few months later and close to this spot, the RUC blocked a march by Queen's University students. They were protesting at the Stormont ban on Queen's University Republican Club. Myself and a republican friend were walking by. Our curiosity aroused by this new spectacle, my friend went to investigate at close quarters. The students staged a sit down. My friend was among those arrested. Subsequently, the Queen's students brought a new force into the slowly fermenting political agitation. Later they would form Peoples Democracy, which would add its own pinch of highly articulate and active ingredients to the civil rights melting pot.

That pot simmered gently until 1968. In the meantime, the remaining months of 1967 were more or less uneventful, that is if you discount the time that "Throw-the-Brick" Morgan threw a brick at the British Queen and her husband as their royal car was escorted down Belfast's Great Victoria Street. As "All you need is love" kept the Beatles at number one in the charts, Ian Paisley threw snowballs at Jack Lynch when he visited Terence O'Neill at Stormont. The day after that event an opinion poll showed that a majority in the 6 counties thought it unnecessary to legislate against discrimination. The civil rights struggle was set to be an uphill one.

The ingredients in the NICRA stew were diverse. They included civil libertarians, who were genuinely affronted by the lack of civil rights in the British state. Their interest was in removing these injustices. Others had a more radical and long-sighted view. They saw the civil rights platform providing a forum for political unity among progressive elements. Some of these saw the successful achievement of the civil rights aims creating a situation where such unity would, in a new democratic set-up, spread to the divided Catholic and Protestant working class, transforming sectarian differences into class unity. And some saw the civil rights struggle as a means of confronting an apartheid state, exposing its contradictions and building popular opposition to them and to the state itself. More because of the nature of the state and the crass stupidity of the London and Stormont governments than through any long-headed political planning or control by any of the above tendencies, that last scenario quickly became the almost inevitable conclusion to what was a modest campaign for reasonable, basic, and just demands.

NICRA in its early days never had a unified strategy for confronting the state with these demands. It was modelled on the British National Council for Civil Liberties and began its existence by almost anonymously collating complaints of civil rights breaches. The leadership was cautious, perhaps rightly so, but the initiative never lay with it anyway. The initiative was on the streets and any campaign which involves street politics needs its leadership on the streets also; otherwise it ceases to lead. NICRA, whose perceived role was to lobby for legislative changes, tried to avoid street politics in the beginning. Then when these developed, almost despite NICRA, and on occasions quite definitely in spite of NICRA, a street leadership, which was already involved in separate campaigns in different parts of the 6 counties, filled the leadership vacuum in these areas.

This development was aided not only by the existence of separate agitations in Derry, Tyrone and Belfast, which had their own local leaderships championing localised campaigns against unfair housing allocation and other injustices, but by the spread of local civil rights committees which were largely autonomous. It was helped too by the reaction of Unionist bullyboys, including the RUC, whose antics moved the whole situation on. As it turned out after 5 October 1968, a strange alliance of soon-to-be SDLP leaders, some of the old guard NICRA leadership, the republican leadership and kindred spirits represented the gradualist tendency, while other republicans, the very energetic Peoples Democracy, and the vast majority of civil rights supporters formed a more combative tendency seeking to expose the contradictions of the 6 county state.

These differences were mirrored within republican ranks. While the Dublin leadership had a clear enough view of the gradualist strategy, their Northern representatives, especially in Belfast, had a hazier view. This was partly a result of the Northern leadership's non-involvement in actual street activity, which permitted a degree of initiative to be wrested from them by rank and file activists who were taking a more realistic attitude than that laid down by the Dublin leadership. It also arose partly as a result of the fluidity of internal republican politics, which had still at that time to gell into the Goulding/MacGiolla leadership line — Cathal Goulding, a senior republican leader, and Tomás MacGiolla, president of Sinn Féin, were leading advocates of the gradualist, reformist politics which culminated in what is now the Workers' Party. The Belfast leadership, which was to toe the Goulding/MacGiolla line in 1969, was in those less dogmatic times advocating or supporting pragmatic and at times, as we have seen, contradictory positions.

Thus there were two separate, if occasionally overlapping agendas being followed by the republicans. One group was intent on exposing the irreformable nature of the 6 county state; the other was following a gradualist approach to reform the state. These elements were at least agreed on the merits of the civil rights campaign. Others, however, were not too sure. The absence of a united Ireland demand, a distrust of "politics" and a fear of reforms — the view that "If the civil rights demands are conceded, people won't want a united Ireland" — manifested itself in much grumbling and sidelines dissent.

More positively, the politicisation of the ailing republican struggle encouraged republican involvement with other forces in hitherto neglected issues, the fruits of which started to appear in the form of well-publicised demonstrations against housing malpractice in Derry and in the Caledon squat in County Tyrone, when republicans helped a local family to occupy a council house which had been allocated to a single young woman who worked for a local Unionist candidate. Nationalist MP Austin Currie (later SDLP) got a lot of publicity for himself when he joined the squat fairly briefly, accompanied by TV cameras, but the groundwork had been done for weeks before by the republicans. (Six years later Currie, as a Minister in the 1974 power-sharing administration, would impose punitive collection charges on people he had encouraged to go on rent and rates strike.) The confrontationist, though passive, nature of these activities, which spread also to Belfast, suited the mood of grassroots republican activists and was highly popular among discontented nationalists. Such activities, added to increasing republican impatience to move ahead on "their own" issues — the ban on Sinn Féin and on open political activity by republicans — also were at odds with the more cautious approach of the NICRA leadership.

The first NICRA protest rallies were held in Newry and Armagh in the spring of 1968 after the banning of an Easter Rising commemoration parade. The first civil rights march took place in August 1968 from Coalisland to Dungannon. Almost 18 months after NICRA was formed, a hesitant beginning to the mass civil rights activity slowly developed. The 5 October march in Derry was to accelerate the process.

The local activists who organized this Derry march sought sponsorship from NICRA and from prominent people in the local community, including John Hume, then a local teacher who was prominent in the Credit Union movement and the campaign for a university for Derry. He refused his support. NICRA reluctantly and belatedly endorsed the march, which was going to go ahead anyway, and Stormont banned it. So it was that, courtesy of television coverage, the world saw the real face of British and Unionist rule in the 6 counties. The RUC smashed into the relatively small demonstration, exposing the brutal nature of Unionist domination and the ruthless denial of basic democratic rights. They split many skulls in the process. Nevertheless, a few weeks later 15,000 people demonstrated in Derry against RUC brutality and NICRA's demands received further widespread publicity. Universal franchise in local elections, an end to gerrymandered boundaries, the repeal of the Special Powers Act, an end to job and housing discrimination, and disbandment of the B Specials fronted the civil rights agenda.

These demands also became a focus for the emerging differences between the republican leadership and some rank and file activists. The leadership position had by now become clearer. The civil rights struggle was not only seen by them as a serious attempt to democratise the state, but to facilitate this process the national question, the issue of Partition, was to be set to one side in order to allay Unionist fears, and the movement was to be demilitarised. This strategy had one serious defect: it underestimated the reactionary and irreformable nature of the state itself and the reluctance of the London government and its Stormont management to introduce reforms. This reality was slowly dawning on many of us who came to believe that the major effect of the civil rights struggle, aside from winning some reforms or partial reforms, would be to show clearly the reactionary and colonial nature of the state and the responsibility of the British government for this situation.

We were also enjoying the breakdown of republican isolation, the political exchanges and interchanges, the pooling of resources and experiences arising from the informal alliances which were being developed in the "thick of battle" between the different elements of the civil rights movement. The traditional internalisation of republican activities and their restriction to a chosen few now seemed a thing of the past and, while the leadership plotted its gradualist approach, we felt, rightly or wrongly, that we were more in touch with reality. For example, Belfast republicans at Duke Street in Derry on 5 October were instructed to push visiting notables into the front line. A sensible instruction, but one which accepted that while attempting to democratise the state there was a need for dramatic confrontations in order to expose what was wrong with it. And these confrontations flatly contradicted the leadership's strategy of avoiding "provocation". They also moved the entire situation on and crystallized tensions within NICRA itself. These became most obvious following Terence O'Neill's "Ulster stands at the crossroads" television broadcast a few weeks after he had announced a five-point reform programme in November 1968.

Civil rights demonstrations had been opposed by loyalist counter-demonstrations, usually led by Ian Paisley; RUC brutality was an occupational hazard for civil rights activists and some B Specials had been fully mobilised by Stormont. In his "crossroads" broadcast O'Neill called for an end to civil disorder and agitation, and support for his reform package. He warned that Westminster might intervene if there was no improvement in the situation. NICRA responded by calling for a period of "truce", without marches or demonstrations.

The NICRA announcement led to much discussion among grassroots activists. Peoples Democracy took the lead when they announced that they would march from Belfast to Derry, beginning on New Year's Day 1969. Initial republican disagreement with this initiative saw a number of us being ordered not to take part. Days later this leadership position was submerged by the boots, bricks and batons of off-duty B Specials and their associates as the RUC led the marchers into the ambush at Burntollet bridge. The Burntollet march showed that the reforms promised by O'Neill and the public relations exercise which followed his announcement were meaningless. It showed that nothing had changed. The British state had certainly not made reforms voluntarily. It would never of its own accord have even begun to move towards doing away with some of the things upon which the very existence of the state depended. Once there was any movement towards removing these, the foundations of the state became insecure. As the old order of things began to crumble, and as the British moved in to prop up their client state, the shortcomings and futility of a gradualist approach became increasingly obvious. Full civil rights and the existence of a partitionist and gerrymandered apartheid state were incompatible.

The struggle for civil rights was developing into a struggle for national rights. Northern republicans, including those in positions of leadership, were forced to reconsider the Goulding leadership's approach. Thus later in January 1969 it was republican stewards who took the initiative, discarded their armbands, and turned with gusto on the RUC at a banned march in Newry. The situation had developed rapidly. The civil rights demands were demands for rights which were taken for granted in Britain and Western Europe. They were simple, modest and moderate, yet they evoked a ferocious response from the state and its supporters. The civil rights movement looked for the democratisation of the 6 county state, but the state made it abundantly clear that it would not and could not implement democratic reforms. The civil rights movement had not demanded the abolition of the state, nor a united Ireland. The civil rights struggle had not raised the constitutional question, but the reaction of the state and the active British intervention in support of the state brought the constitutional question to the fore, and the existence of the 6 county state into question.

Parallel with this, the republican strategy of organizing politically to achieve democracy within the state, which had involved a turning away from the physical force tradition, had run headlong into the reality of the irreformable sectarian state. It was a reality which the republican leadership was totally unprepared for and as the crisis within the state deepened, differences within republican ranks were exacerbated by events and by the return of some lapsed members who had disagreed with the general direction of the movement and who had been absent during the politicisation period. Under these pressures the loosely united tendencies which made up the republican movement came sharply into conflict. This would have occurred anyway, in time, because of the underlying strategic and ideological strains, but the civil rights struggle and the backlash from the August 1969 pogroms in Belfast dictated the timing and to a large degree the sharpness of the divisions. Latent personality conflicts were given a new vigour by the emotive events of 14-15 August 1969 — the attacks on the Catholic areas of the Falls Road, Clonard and Ardoyne — which saw the biggest forced movement of population in any part of Western Europe since the Second World War, as Catholics fled from a state backlash which saw entire streets burned out and left eight people dead (six Catholics and two Protestants). The ramifications of those events affected all of Ireland.

The Goulding/MacGiolla leadership had got it wrong. Their failure to provide adequate defence, allied to the mishandling of an almost unprecedented opportunity to move the entire situation on was bad enough. But when circumstances dictated and cried out for a leadership capable of unifying, or encouraging the maximum unity of progressives, anti-imperialists, socialists, republicans and nationalists, the republican leadership dithered and the republican movement divided. As the institutions of the Northern state tottered, both republican factions rushed belatedly to procure weapons. The political ground was left untilled, creating a vacuum which was later to be filled by a generally unchallenged SDLP. That the entire movement turned at this time to armed resistance was not entirely due to any ingrained militarism, but had everything to do with the stark reality of the situation.

That reality continues to this day. The British state in the north-east of Ireland is a failed political entity and since 1969 it has been kept in existence by a life-support unit of British occupation forces. The logic behind the Goulding/MacGiolla error on the national question has also continued through to this day in the pseudo-socialist posturings and at times two-nationist and partitionist approach of the Workers' Party. The republican movement also suffers from a legacy today, especially in the 26 counties, which is directly attributable to the distrust of "politics" which intensified in reaction to the Goulding/MacGiolla era. Only now is an increasingly politicised Sinn Féin attempting to recoup lost ground.

Now that we have reached the 20th anniversary of the civil rights struggle, the denials of democratic rights continue. They were rediscovered in the wake of the 1980-81 Armagh and H Blocks hunger strikes by the Irish establishment, who played no part in the original civil rights struggle and ignored the Northern crisis until it was forced upon them. These denials of democratic rights — "the causes of alienation" — were to be erased, we were assured, by the 1985 Hillsborough Treaty, or Anglo-Irish Agreement. But mentioning these issues in cosy chats at the intergovernmental meetings established under the Hillsborough Treaty has had no effect on the British. The inequities remain and there is ample proof in the recent past of British willingness to intensify them. There is a need today as there was in the '60s for a campaign for democratic rights in the 6 counties. The right to vote for which we marched and were batoned, and for which people died, has been eroded by British legislation. We were to learn that unless we cast our votes in accordance with the wishes of the British government, that government had little regard for the results of the ballot box. Thus after Bobby Sands was elected to Westminster in April 1981, while on hunger strike, the British government introduced legislation to ban prisoner candidates, and when Sinn Féin won electoral support, the British declared that they would not meet or accept representations from Sinn Féin's elected representatives. When this disenfranchising of Sinn Féin voters was seen to have little effect on Sinn Féin's support in subsequent elections, restrictive and undemocratic obstacles were introduced for voters in the form of compulsory identity requirements (e.g. a driving licence or a passport). As this also had little effect and as the Sinn Féin vote remains remarkably solid, at the time of writing the British government is preparing a compulsory electoral pledge for candidates designed to try to prevent Sinn Féin from contesting elections.

British injustice continues in other areas also. Discrimination in employment and employment opportunity continues. Coercive legislation of the most brutal kind remains. The UDR has replaced the B Specials — a change only of name and uniform — and the RUC remains as sectarian as before, just becoming more numerous, more murderous and better equipped since 1969. They are ably aided today by a British army occupation force. This is what keeps the 6 county state intact; without them it would not survive.

The present "unity by consent" formula is a fudge — a catch 22 — which shifts the terms of the debate about Partition away from Britain's intransigence, and puts the responsibility for the British connection on the Unionists. But of course it is not loyalty or love for the Unionists which keeps the British government in Ireland. Even my friends in the Ark Bar knew that. British policy is a failed policy, that much is clear. What is needed is for the British government to change its current policy to one of ending Partition and the Union in the context of Irish reunification. That means withdrawing from Ireland and handing over sovereignty to an all-Ireland government.

The Unionists have no right of veto over the unification of Ireland and the ending of the British connection. That is a matter of principle. But all sensible people agree that the consent of Northern Protestants is desirable on the constitutional, financial and political arrangements needed to replace Partition. Northern Protestants have fears about their civil and religious liberties, and these liberties must rightly be guaranteed and protected. We who are denied our civil rights do not seek to deny these rights to others. What is needed is a regime of equality shaped by the diverse elements which make up our nation. The British government can play an influential role in persuading members of the Unionist tradition that their best interests lie with the rest of the Irish people in building a new all-Ireland society. They can start that process by ending the Unionist veto. While it remains, the Unionists have no real incentive to examine any other option.

The important, crucial and most fundamental step is of course that the British government change its current policy. It will do this more speedily if it can no longer count on support from Dublin and the SDLP, and if it is faced with pressure from Dublin, supported by the international goodwill which Ireland enjoys and which we can enlist to support the Irish cause. Alongside such a strategy, which should include an international and diplomatic offensive by the Dublin government, there is an urgent need to win improvements on the ground on the issue of democratic rights. This calls for firm pressure on Britain and a campaign of international lobbying and publicity coupled with national political activity. By such means will Britain be forced to end the use of plastic bullets, strip searching, Crown forces' brutality, ill-treatment of prisoners, and torture in interrogation centres, and to change its attitude towards the repatriation of prisoners, the release of the SOSPs (prisoners serving indefinite sentences at "the Secretary of State's Pleasure"), discrimination in employment and high nationalist unemployment, the Prevention of Terrorism Act, reviews of life sentences, and cultural rights.

Of course, Dublin would be better able to pursue such objectives if it was free from criticism itself on similar issues. An array of repressive legislation, mostly based on British laws and including the obnoxious Offences Against the State Act, should be repealed. Similarly the non-jury Special Criminal Court should be abolished. Protestations by Dublin about unjust British special powers are little more than the pot calling the kettle black — a cynical exercise in the politics of illusion, refined and institutionalised by Hillsborough. If Dublin is genuinely concerned about, for example, the rights of prisoners in British jails, then it should end indeterminate sentences for life prisoners in Portlaoise Prison. These prisoners should be given release dates, and Don O'Leary, serving four years in Portlaoise for possession of a poster, should be released. Censorship laws, notably Section 31 of the

Broadcasting Act, should be scrapped. Extradition should end. Some of the Irish taxpayers' money now used to maintain Partition should be used to fund a European Court of Human Rights appeal by the Birmingham Six or to set up an international tribunal on their case and those of the Guildford Four and the Maguire family. The British government needs to be taught to respect the rights of Irish citizens. The education of the British government in this regard must start with us standing up for our rights and insisting that our public representatives do likewise.

The Irish establishment has failed not only to secure the most basic rights of citizens in the six counties but also to guarantee the rights of citizens in their own jurisdiction. Forced emigration and unemployment, cut backs in housing, health and education, archaic social legislation and the sell out of Irish culture are also part of the legacy of Partition. The struggle for democracy must include the disparate victims of Partition in both parts of Ireland and a national struggle must be forged which fuses social, economic and cultural discontent within a campaign for national self-determination.

Such a policy will ensure a permanent peace in the North and an end to sectarianism and division there. It will also advance the economic, spiritual and social welfare of this nation and initiate the healing process which we all deserve and desire. Twenty years after the start of the civil rights struggle is that too much to ask?

LONG MARCH
TO FREEDOM

Michael Farrell was born in Magherafelt, County Derry, in 1944 and educated at St Patrick's College, Armagh, Queen's University, Belfast, and the University of Strathclyde, Glasgow. A founder member of Peoples Democracy and organizer of the PD march to Derry in January 1969, he contested the Northern Ireland general election of 1969 against Prime Minister Terence O'Neill and Reverend Ian Paisley. A member of the NICRA executive from 1969 to 1970, he continued to be active in Peoples Democracy until 1980 and since then has been involved in civil liberties campaigns. He is the author of *Northern Ireland the Orange State*, *Arming the Protestants* and *Sheltering the Fugitive*. He is married and has two children.

Our busload of students and Young Socialists was half an hour late getting into Derry on Saturday 5 October 1968. The civil rights march, banned by Home Affairs Minister William Craig, had already set off and been stopped by grim-faced rows of RUC men after about 200 yards. The marchers were holding a meeting and Betty Sinclair, chairperson of the Northern Ireland Civil Rights Association (NICRA), was telling the crowd that they had made their protest and it was time to go home peacefully.

We were not having that. It was 1968, the year of student revolutions in Paris and Prague, of Mexico City and the Chicago Democratic Convention. We did not think of ourselves in quite that league but going home peacefully meant letting Bill Craig and the RUC walk all over us. We would have been angrier still if we had known that the RUC had already attacked the head of the march, batoning Gerry Fitt MP and Eddie McAteer, leader of the opposition in the Stormont parliament, and the leaders' response had been the meeting and the plea to go home. We only heard all that afterwards.

Our group of 30 or 40 protesters pushed to the front and up against the RUC. We did not attack them. In fact we lectured them about gerrymandering and how they were being exploited by the Unionist bosses too, and then we appealed to them to let us march. But we intended to stay put: if they wanted us to go home they would have to make us.

Suddenly an RUC man rammed a baton into the belly of the man beside me. I did not even see the baton that hit me on the head and the next few minutes were hazy. I only know that in the TV film of the events I can be seen on the ground being belaboured by an RUC officer with a blackthorn stick. After that it was chaos. RUC men charged wildly about batoning everyone in sight, including Saturday afternoon shoppers who had stopped to watch out of curiosity. Then came a water cannon, the first time it had been used in Ireland or Britain. Orla, my wife, got arrested and bundled into a police jeep while a couple of more street-wise comrades pulled me up a laneway, switched my jacket for another one and got me to hospital. Meanwhile Orla was released. The RUC did not know what to do with women protesters at that stage.

Derry dominated the TV news all over the weekend. The effect was electric, especially among students. This was our Paris, our Prague, our Chicago. Later we would learn that marches had been batoned off the streets of Derry regularly in the 1950s, but there had been no TV then and meanwhile expectations had changed. We did not know our place the way our parents did. Three thousand students marched in Belfast four days after the events in Derry, only to be stopped by the RUC as well. The students, from what had been the most docile campus in Western Europe throughout the 1960s, were not ready for confrontation. They sat down for hours in front of the RUC lines and then trudged back to the university. But even that apparent defeat was turned into victory. The students were angry and that night an emotional mass meeting set up a campaigning movement: Peoples Democracy. Our Young Socialist group became its hard core. We hardly spent a night at home for the next few months — or years, if it comes to that.

There was an explosion of energy, enthusiasm and vitality. Posters and leaflets appeared as if from nowhere. Itinerant groups of Peoples Democracy members would turn up in the most unlikely and unwelcoming places across the 6 counties of Northern Ireland to spread the message and try to set up civil rights committees. School students defied teachers and nuns to hold Peoples Democracy meetings. We occupied the parliament buildings at Stormont and the Unionist government did not know what to do with us. Peoples Democracy was only one strand in the civil rights movement but it provided much of its colour and drive. It had all the naïvety and arrogance of youth, of the first generation to benefit from post-war British education reforms and of the first generation not to be cowed by memories of the pogroms of the '20s and the depression of the '30s. Peoples Democracy members did things their parents would not have attempted because that generation knew from bitter experience that it would not be allowed to get away with them. Yet these actions had to be taken, or attempted, so as to demonstrate the nature of the sectarian state in Northern Ireland.

We were as a result in constant conflict with the cautious, middle-class leadership of the Northern Ireland Civil Rights Association — supported, ironically, by the couple of Communist Party members on the NICRA executive — who were always afraid of going too far and half astonished that they had been let go as far as they had done. When the Unionist Prime Minister, Terence O'Neill, announced a few half-hearted reforms and called for a "truce" in December 1968, the NICRA leaders jumped at the chance. But once again we in Peoples Democracy, or at least in its Young Socialist hard core, were not having that. O'Neill was not going to be let off the hook so easily. He must be forced to grant one man, one vote (that was before the feminist revolution) and break with the Unionist backwoodsmen, or the British government must be forced to do it over his head. We decided to march from Belfast to Derry in January 1969.

The whole civil rights movement drew inspiration from the black civil rights movement in the United States. Its anthem was "We Shall Overcome" (though we preferred "The Internationale") and at the first march from Coalisland to Dungannon in August 1968 one of the speakers had declared to loud applause: "We are the white negroes of Northern Ireland". We in the Young Socialists/Peoples Democracy identified particularly with the younger, more radical Student Non-Violent Coordinating Committee (SNCC) who like us were in regular conflict with the older, more cautious leaders of Martin Luther King's Southern Christian Leadership Conference. But King and SNCC chairman John Lewis had marched together from Selma to Montgomery in Alabama in 1965, and the violence of the racist state troopers who blocked that march had caused such outrage across the US that President Lyndon Johnson had been forced to push through the Voting Rights Act. The march to Derry was modelled on the Selma-Montgomery march and we hoped it would have a similar effect. A lot of the route was through my home area of South Derry so I knew, or thought I knew, the likely reaction — but it turned out to be a bit worse than I expected. The Young Socialist Alliance pushed the decision to march to Derry and we also tried to push the civil rights movement to the left by calling it, like its US model, a Civil Rights and Anti-Poverty march and calling on Protestant workers to join in. We prepared leaflets giving the number of houses without flush toilets or running water in the villages along the route, but that aspect of things got swamped after the Burntollet ambush.

Three episodes stick in my mind from that march. On the second day as we left the tiny nationalist village of Toome our route was blocked yet again by the RUC, who forced us up country lanes and backroads on the usual pretext that the main road was blocked by loyalist vigilantes. But standing behind the RUC on the main road to make sure that they stopped us was senior Stormont Minister and local MP James Chichester Clark. A few months later he was to succeed Terence O'Neill as Prime Minister of Northern Ireland. If that was the attitude of a prominent "moderate" Unionist leader, it was clear that the Stormont government was not going to make concessions of its own free will.

But also as we left Toome, an old woman stepped out from a run-down cottage and handed me a packet of ten cigarettes — as much as she could afford — "to keep you going on the way". And that afternoon as we passed a farmhouse gate on a deserted stretch of country road, another woman came out and handed me a bag of sandwiches. "I heard on the radio they'd stopped you going the main road and I made these in case you came this way," she said. They were just two of hundreds of spontaneous gifts and gestures of support that we got all along the route of that march.

Then came Burntollet. At a crossroads as we left Claudy, County Derry, on the last day of the march, the RUC officer in charge halted us for the umpteenth time. He called me over. There were some loyalists ahead in a field beside the road, he said. They might throw a few stones but he thought we would get through if we kept close in to the hedge on the right-hand side of the road — it was up to us. For once the RUC were not trying to re-route us. The marchers had no doubts: we would carry on. It never occurred to me to wonder why the RUC had not tried to stop us this time.

As we went downhill a narrow lane hidden by the hedge joined the road on the right-hand side just before Burntollet bridge. Suddenly a crowd of loyalists armed with sticks and clubs burst out on us. I didn't see much of it. I put my head down and pushed and shoved as many marchers as I could past the attackers. Once through I concentrated on getting the marchers up the hill on the other side and forming up again. Some were hysterical and screaming. Some had been badly beaten, others had been driven down into the river Faughan and were soaked through. Some thought others had been left behind at the mercy of the loyalist attackers. I went back down to the bridge to check. There were no marchers left but dozens of loyalists with armbands and cudgels were standing around chatting to groups of RUC men and having a smoke after their exertions.

Our job was to get to Derry. We pressed on, to be attacked twice more before we got into the city. I didn't see the last attack. I had got knocked out in a fusillade of stones and petrol bombs at the loyalist Irish Street estate on the outskirts of the city. It was only when the march was all over that I realised what had happened at Burntollet. The RUC, commanded by senior officers, had led us straight into an ambush which they must have known about in advance, and had then had a friendly chat with the ambushers afterwards. It was a good example of just how deeply ingrained sectarianism was in the whole structure of the Northern Ireland state. There was quite literally one law for us and another for our loyalist attackers, many of whom turned out to be off-duty members of the Special Constabulary, the B Specials. The civil rights movement had set out with very modest demands: one man, one vote, an end to religious discrimination, repeal of the Special Powers Act, and disbanding of the entirely Protestant B Specials. The demands had seemed too modest to us in the Young Socialists and Peoples Democracy but the Northern state had resisted them like a threat to its very existence and had allowed, not to say encouraged, loyalist vigilantes to harass and hinder us at every turn.

Peoples Democracy marched, picketed, organized and protested all through 1969. In February we even stood in a snap general election called by Terence O'Neill. We worried whether we were compromising too much with the bourgeois parliamentary system and consoled ourselves by picking unwinnable seats — I stood against the Prime Minister and Ian Paisley in Bannside. We did quite well, nearly too well. To our consternation, one of our candidates almost got elected. We held a march to Dublin that Easter under the slogan "Tories Out, North and South" to protest at bad housing, unemployment, repressive legislation and the bans on divorce and contraceptives in the South. And in May Peoples Democracy member Bernadette Devlin was elected to Westminster for her home constituency of Mid-Ulster. Then we were confounded. Ultra-leftism about parliament and our own loose structure meant we did not know what to do with an MP. The result was confusion and some resentment between Peoples Democracy and its new MP.

But then came the Battle of the Bogside in August 1969 when local people in Derry, aided by the new street-fighting MP for Mid-Ulster, fought for two days and nights with stones and petrol bombs to keep the RUC from invading their area after a march by the Unionist Apprentice Boys organization. The RUC had already terrorised the area several times since the beginning of the year. This time the Bogsiders won and the British government had to send in troops to restore the Stormont regime's crumbling authority. However, Belfast suffered for

Derry's temporary victory. On the night the British troops appeared in Derry, the RUC, the B Specials and armed loyalists attacked the Catholic area of the Falls Road in Belfast. Armoured cars drove up and down the road spraying it with machine-gun fire. Loyalist mobs, following the RUC and Specials, burned out 150 Catholic houses between the Falls and Shankill roads. A handful of IRA members tried to fight back. Five people were killed: four Catholics, one a nine-year-old boy, and one Protestant.

I saw a large number of RUC men arrive at Hastings Street barracks at the bottom of the Falls Road that night, then I left to collect a pirate radio transmitter Peoples Democracy were aiming to set up in the area. We couldn't get back into the Lower Falls and we could not stay at home (we lived near the university) lest the RUC raid us or the loyalists attack — or both. Instead we stayed in Andersonstown at the top of the Falls Road, hearing the machine guns firing for what seemed like hours. The RUC did arrive at our house that night but left empty handed. In other places a number of republicans and civil rights leaders were arrested and held without trial under the Special Powers Act. Next day we went back to the Lower Falls and caught the tail end of that night of terror. As we walked up Albert Street a loyalist gunman was sniping down the narrow streets from the roof of a nearby mill. Most of the street was safe enough if you kept close in to the doorways, but there was one entry where he had a clear line of fire and you just had to duck and run. The whole thing seemed unreal and the gunfire like that of a toy pistol. Soon afterwards local youths petrol bombed the building and the gunman beat a retreat.

That afternoon British troops appeared on the Falls Road, though Bombay Street in the Clonard area and Ardoyne had still to undergo another attack before the troops moved in. The civil rights movement, including Peoples Democracy and the Republican Clubs/IRA, had not anticipated this — that the state and loyalist militants would turn their guns on residential areas and Catholic homes would be burned out in a combined act of revenge and intimidation. The RUC and the Stormont government had reintroduced the gun to Northern politics and we had no strategy to deal with it. The nationalists were crying out for defence and the demand was urgent enough to send MPs for the nationalist areas scurrying to Dublin looking for arms, and to involve Dublin Ministers and the Irish army in moves to supply them. Ironically some of the MPs who drove back with their car boots full of everything from .22 rifles to shotguns to submachine guns, were later to be among the loudest in denouncing the use of violence. For the IRA's part, the attacks on the ghettos and the organization's failure to defend them discredited its leadership and led to the split into Provisionals and Officials. And because the old leadership was identified with the politicisation and move to the left by the republican movement, the new Provisional movement was marked by a deep distrust of politics and a renewed emphasis on physical force pure and simple.

August 1969 marked a turning point in the civil rights campaign. Where it had begun by demanding modest reforms from the Stormont government, after August few nationalists or Catholics believed that even those demands could or would be granted by a Stormont administration. We in Peoples Democracy began to raise the demand to smash or suspend Stormont and it gradually won wider support, though bitterly opposed by Official Sinn Féin. We had little interest in unity with the Southern Irish state, which was just as socially conservative as the Northern one, and hoped that the fight against sectarianism would unite the working class, Protestant and Catholic, North and South. Dismantling sectarianism turned out to be a lot harder than we had expected but we became more and more convinced that class unity and socialism could not be achieved until we had done so.

Most Northern nationalists still wanted to see a united Ireland eventually, but by the 1960s that had become a fairly distant objective. Many thought a dismantling of Orange rule in the North would lead to a united Ireland in the long run. But nationalists also wanted an improvement in their present conditions, and wanted that much more urgently. Most of them welcomed the British troops when they appeared on the streets, and looked to Westminster to remedy their grievances. At first it looked as if Westminster might; "Sunny Jim" Callaghan, the British Home Secretary, toured the Bogside in Derry and listened to the Catholics' complaints. When Harold Wilson, the Labour Prime Minister, announced the disbandment of the B Specials, hardly anyone noticed that they were to be replaced by the Ulster Defence Regiment (UDR).

The nationalists' honeymoon with the British army did not last long. The British troops were there to aid the civil power — and perhaps restrain some of its wilder excesses — but not to overthrow it. And the civil power was still the Stormont government which would not make any more concessions and demanded a tougher and tougher security policy. The British troops were inexorably drawn into confrontation with the disaffected youth of the nationalist ghettos. And the newly formed Provisional IRA moved equally inexorably from defence, to retaliation for British army brutality, to offensive action. They talked now of fighting for the old demand — a united Ireland. But that was still a minority view, even within the nationalist minority. Most nationalists saw the way to a united Ireland — or a socialist republic — through making demands on the British government to dismantle the sectarian state in the North.

There were different ways of posing those demands, however. We in Peoples Democracy and the republicans of both varieties were still on the streets protesting, though increasingly in reaction to repression by the authorities rather than on our own agenda. But the old unity of the civil rights movement was breaking up. The respectable middle-class elements, never at ease on the streets, were encouraged by the Dublin government and the British Labour leadership to see an opening for themselves in parliamentary and constitutional politics and began setting up the SDLP. They opposed any return to the streets and wanted all protests channeled through constitutional means, i.e. through themselves.

There was fragmentation in another direction as well. There had been a significant number of Protestants in the early Peoples Democracy and the civil rights movement had a certain amount of liberal Protestant support. Both dwindled as the situation became more polarised and as the whole nature of the Northern state was brought into question. Liberals gave up or joined the newly formed Alliance Party, an amalgam of upper-class do-gooders and lower class social climbers. Life became well nigh impossible for Protestant civil rights activists as loyalist paramilitary groups began to dominate Protestant areas. 1969-70 saw the rise of a number of armed loyalist groups, formed to defend Protestant supremacy and the Northern state. With a sectarian populist ideology and uneasy links with the security forces they resembled similar groups in the 1920s which had later been absorbed into the Special Constabulary. They also had a passing resemblance to the Blackshirts and Brownshirts of the 1920s and 1930s. In the early '70s these loyalist paramilitaries launched a horrific campaign of sectarian assassinations of Catholic civilians as retaliation for

IRA attacks.

Yet for all the rising tension there was a curious interregnum in 1970-71. While military and sectarian violence grew and Peoples Democracy was heavily involved in protesting against it, we were still trying to build links with sections of the Protestant working class, ranging from leafletting the shipyard and the aircraft factory in East Belfast to picketing the Belfast Lord Mayor's shop in the Protestant heartland of the Shankill Road over increases in city bus fares. We actually got some support amidst all the abuse outside the Lord Mayor's shop one Saturday afternoon, but in the end we had to beat a retreat. When I looked at the street name where we had parked our car I discovered we were in Malvern Street, where the first loyalist killings of modern times had taken place in 1966. That night an RUC Special Branch officer came to warn me that the UVF planned to shoot me if I went back to the Shankill Road. How did he know so quickly? I reflected afterwards, and if the RUC were so well informed about the UVF's plans how come they could not do more about it than simply warn their potential victims?

The introduction of internment without trial in August 1971 put an end to the interregnum. Six months earlier Prime Minister Chichester Clark had announced that his government was at war with the Provisional IRA. Now it seemed as if both they and the British government had declared war on most of the nationalist minority as well. Five months later they confirmed that impression when the British army shot dead 13 unarmed protesters in Derry on Bloody Sunday. After Bloody Sunday Stormont was dead. The whole nationalist community was in revolt; British army war veterans sent back their medals, the most respectable Catholics resigned from public boards. In a moment of emotion the normally cautious John Hume declared: "It's a united Ireland now or nothing".

I was interned briefly in 1971, and saw some of the men who had been subjected to sensory deprivation by the British army — Britain was later found guilty of inhuman and degrading treatment of them by the European Court of Human Rights — rejoin their colleagues. I knew one of them well. He was in his thirties and had canvassed for me when I had stood in the Northern Ireland general election of February 1969. But when Pat Shivers came into the prison exercise yard one morning, I did not recognise him. He was a stooped old man. He died prematurely as a result of his treatment. I discovered also that two of my fellow internees had first been imprisoned in the 1920s. Many had been there in the 1940s and a lot more in the 1950s, mostly without trial. Sons were interned with fathers who had done several stints before, uncles with nephews. My internment gave me a new insight into the weight of repression the nationalist community had suffered over the years and the endurance and resilience of the republican tradition even if its political thinking had often been limited.

On the outside time and again I met families who had been burnt out in 1969-70 and whose parents or grandparents had been burnt out as well in 1935 or in the '20s. They had a deep-rooted feeling of insecurity in the Northern state and an inbred distrust of the RUC and British army that recent events had honed into downright hatred. Living in Andersonstown after 1971 but teaching in the Belfast College of Technology, the city's major centre for craft and apprentice training, I began to see the extent and effect of job discrimination at first hand. Unemployment in areas of Catholic West Belfast was well over 60% while my classes in skilled crafts like mechanical, electrical and aeronautical engineering were 80 to 90% Protestant. Shipwrights were usually 100% Protestant. Discrimination had been a fairly abstract grievance to me until then, but now I could see its effect on families where no one had worked for a couple of generations and had no expectations of finding work either. Later on the Fair Employment Agency was to put statistics on those impressions — the main contribution of a watchdog that never managed to bite. And on top of all that was the daily or nightly toll of raids, arrests, beatings, harassment, abuse and jailings on a community effectively under military occupation. Only the colour of the uniforms varied with the ebb and flow of attempts to Ulsterise the conflict by replacing the British army with the RUC.

The nationalist/Catholic community wanted equal access to jobs, an end to seemingly never-ending repression, and a feeling of security: that they would not be attacked in their homes or at work, if they had jobs, by loyalist mobs or gunmen, or that the security forces would protect them if they were. And they wanted some access to political power and recognition of their cultural and political identity. More and more they felt they could not achieve those aims within the Northern Ireland state, even under British Direct Rule. Irish unity, or at least some form of Dublin involvement, was back on the political agenda, not as an abstract dream but as a practical necessity for the nationalist community.

The British suspended Stormont in March 1972 and instituted

Direct Rule, but a sizeable minority of the nationalist community now had no faith in British intentions and saw British withdrawal as a necessary prelude to any solution. And of course British withdrawal did not seem so impossible when the British themselves flew the leadership of the Provisional IRA to London to meet the Secretary of State for the North in the summer of 1972, even if little came of those talks. But when a power-sharing Executive composed of Unionists, Alliance Party and SDLP was set up in January 1974 with a commitment as well to a Council of Ireland, many even in the ranks of Provo supporters gave it the benefit of the doubt. It was as traumatic for nationalists to see Catholics or nationalists in a Stormont cabinet after 50 years as it was for the Unionists. However, when the Executive was brought down by a junta of Unionist politicians and loyalist paramilitary groups without the British government raising a hand to save it, nationalists were bitterly disillusioned.

The British would not stand up to the Unionists even to implement a plan of their own devising. The SDLP went greener in reaction and increasingly looked to Dublin for support. Provo supporters — and there were more of them now — were confirmed in their desire for a British withdrawal and their belief that only the bomb and the bullet would secure it. The mid-'70s was a grim time. The British concentrated on a military solution and turned a blind eye to loyalist paramilitary gangs who were carrying out a horrific sectarian murder campaign. The Provos retaliated, though on a smaller scale, and Belfast was gripped by a climate of terror.

Political protest was virtually impossible. The Northern Ireland Civil Rights Association was dead. Peoples Democracy dwindled to a tiny ginger group. Infected with the hysteria that prevailed in the ghettos after the collapse of Sunningdale, we thought a loyalist takeover was imminent and were wrapped up in an ultra-leftist phase of boycotting elections and scorning "reformist" campaigns. The Official republicans, who had abandoned their military campaign in 1972, distanced themselves more and more from any nationalist demands and their whole politics appeared to be based on denouncing the Provos. In the winter of 1974-75 some of their members, led by the charismatic Seamus Costello, left to form the more republican IRSP/INLA and there was an immediate and bitter feud between the IRSP and the Official IRA. Meanwhile the Provos were engaged in a reckless commercial bombing campaign that took a heavy toll of civilian life. Provisional

Sinn Féin was just a support group for the IRA, conservative on social issues, wedded to abstentionism, and unwilling to work with anyone who did not give total support to the armed struggle.

It was impossible in that climate to build a united campaign even within the nationalist community and even on issues like repression. The last attempt, the Political Hostages Release Committee (PHRC), brought together both republican groups, Peoples Democracy and the remnants of NICRA in 1973, but a punch-up between Official and Provo supporters at a rally in August 1973 led to the departure of the Officials and NICRA. A year later Provisional Sinn Féin attacked Peoples Democracy for failing to support the military campaign and the PHRC finally collapsed. Meanwhile social, economic and gender issues were pushed aside even within the ghettos, never mind across the sectarian divide.

There was a bleak war of attrition marked by SAS killings and torture and beatings of republican suspects by the RUC to obtain confessions. The IRA was gradually worn down, though they were never as close to defeat as the Labour Secretary for the North, Roy Mason, used to regularly proclaim. And even if they had been temporarily crushed, that period left such a legacy of bitterness and alienation that they would have sprung up anew in a couple of years.

By the end of the 1970s attrition had left the nationalist community cowed and sullen, though not broken. Small things began to revive the morale of the militant hard core and re-established the tradition of political protest. Peoples Democracy staged a repeat of the Burntollet march in January 1979, the first time a republican protest had been carried outside the ghettos for five or six years. And Bernadette (Devlin) McAliskey stood in the first EEC direct elections in 1979 and got 34,000 votes, enough to shake British propaganda claims that militant republicanism had no support, but few enough to show that it was at a fairly low ebb. Both campaigns had focused on the plight of republican prisoners on the blanket and dirty protest in Long Kesh for political status. And ironically both had been opposed by Sinn Féin, caught up in its own cul-de-sac of non-recognition of the institutions of state. Then came the 1981 hunger strike. The vast majority of nationalists, even if they did not support the IRA, believed they were the product of years of Unionist oppression, backed up by British troops whenever the Unionists got themselves into difficulties. They had no doubt that the hunger strikers were political prisoners. And the courage of the ten young men who were willing to die on hunger strike rebutted years of propaganda claims that the IRA were just cowards and criminals.

The hunger strike inspired a new generation of nationalist youth who had been too young to feel the terror of the mid-'70s and the sectarian assassinations, and rekindled the enthusiasm of people worn out by earlier struggles. It generated something of the spirit of the early civil rights movement; there was a similar excitement and spontaneity, vividly expressed in the spate of folk-art wall paintings in nationalist areas. And that feeling expressed itself at the polls when Bobby Sands was elected in Fermanagh/South Tyrone in April 1981 with a total which clearly included a sizeable number of SDLP votes.

It was confirmed by Bobby Sands' funeral, the biggest nationalist gathering in the North since just after Bloody Sunday. And it was reaffirmed when the relatively unknown Owen Carron was easily elected in Sands' place. The hunger strike had an impact in the South of Ireland reminiscent of August 1969 and Bloody Sunday as two Long Kesh prisoners were elected to Dáil Éireann, bringing about inter alia the fall of Charles Haughey's government.

Ten hunger strikers died and the protest ended without a clear victory on their five demands, but Mrs Thatcher's intransigence had hardened nationalist anger and the experience of mass protest and of fighting elections propelled the Provos into politics. A new leadership emerged in Sinn Féin, the product of the first waves of IRA members to be jailed in the 1970s, and who had acquired in prison the political education they had not had the chance to get outside. They had learned too that there was no simple military victory to be won, that they could not succeed without the active support of the people. In a series of elections between 1982 and 1985 Sinn Féin scored considerable political successes, getting a peak of 102,701 votes — or almost 43% of the combined SDLP/Sinn Féin vote — and winning one seat in the Westminster parliament (June 1983), five seats in a short-lived local Northern assembly which both they and the SDLP boycotted (October 1982), and 59 seats on local councils, which gave them the chair for a time on two councils — Fermanagh and Omagh.

By then the nationalist community had become more polarised, however. One effect of direct British rule which had gradually become more evident was the extension of patronage, jobs and contracts to the Catholic middle class. Catholic builders, contractors, lawyers, administrators were making money under British rule. The Dallas-style mansions of the nouveau riche were spreading on the outskirts of Derry and Newry and wealthy Catholics were buying property in the traditional playground of the Belfast bourgeoisie along the north County Down coast. On the other hand the deepening economic recession was hitting the Catholic working class harder than ever. As overall unemployment soared, Catholics remained two and a half times more likely to be unemployed than Protestants, with overall Catholic male unemployment at 35% in the mid-'80s and double that in the worst affected areas. The unemployment rate for women was lower as fewer women were in the labour market in the male-dominated Northern Ireland society, but the sectarian breakdown was similar. The marginal sectors of the economy where Catholics had found jobs, like construction, were the most vulnerable to the recession, while Protestant control of the manufacturing and engineering sectors tightened. Within the hard core ghettos like West Belfast and the Bogside and Creggan in Derry unemployment had become a way of life.

The SDLP was pulled in two directions. The influential Catholic nouveau riche were happy with the status quo, though some of the younger element were keen on power-sharing devolution within the North so they could get ministerial jobs. The working class hated the status quo and wanted movement towards a united Ireland, or at least some form of joint authority with Dublin. And Sinn Féin was working hard to garner the working-class vote. The SDLP was forced to boycott the new Stormont Assembly set up in 1982 and Dublin, frightened that the SDLP might be replaced by Sinn Féin, was forced to set up the New Ireland Forum in 1983 and press the British for some role in administering the North. The result was the Anglo-Irish Agreement in November 1985 which Dublin and the SDLP sold as "joint authority in all but name", but which Mrs Thatcher clearly saw — and sees — as primarily a vehicle for increased security co-operation. The Unionists were outraged and in a sense, of course, the Agreement was another admission that the old days of Unionist hegemony were gone for good. Nationalists, bowled over by the thought of Southern officials in an office near Stormont monitoring the British administration, and influenced by the Unionists' apoplexy, were pleased. The SDLP vote went up and they won two more seats at Westminster.

But three years on the Anglo-Irish Agreement, in mid-1988, was in a sorry state. It had delivered none of the benefits broadly hinted at at the time — abolition of the UDR, mixed Garda-RUC policing in the North, Southern judges in Northern courts — and in a series of decisions at the start of 1988 the British had seemed to be almost going out of their way to demonstrate its ineffectiveness through their handling of the Stalker/Sampson inquiry, the Birmingham Six case, the release and re-instatement in the British army of a soldier convicted of murder, the Gibraltar shooting of three unarmed IRA members. At the same time the Dublin government and by implication the SDLP had been drawn into closer and closer security co-operation with the RUC, UDR and British army. And the scheduled renegotiation of the Agreement at the end of 1988 looked unlikely to move closer to real joint authority in the North. On the contrary, all the signs are that it is likely to involve concessions to the Unionists such as a voice in the Anglo-Irish Conference or a move towards devolution.

So, 20 years from 1968 and 2,700 deaths later, have the nationalists in Northern Ireland gained their demands; has it all been a failure; or, as some commentators have claimed, did "men of violence" hijack a peaceful movement that had every prospect of success and pervert it to their own ends?

One man (and one woman) one vote has been achieved — though the larger gerrymander of the Northern Ireland state remains. Housing is allocated reasonably fairly though there is still a housing shortage, especially in Greater West Belfast. The B Specials have been disbanded — but they have been replaced by their sons in the UDR and the RUC Reserve. The Special Powers Act has been replaced by the Emergency Provisions Act and the Prevention of Terrorism Act. A Fair Employment Agency was set up in 1976 but eleven years later a British government discussion paper had to admit that "the message of equality of opportunity in employment does not appear to be making a significant impact in relation to any dimension".

For working-class Catholics there has been little real improvement in their conditions and the last two decades have brought an enormous additional burden as thousands of young men and women have spent their youth in prison and/or have been tortured or brutalised by the security forces. There have been tens of thousands of screening arrests and hundreds of thousands of house searches. There have been "shoot to kill" policies, supergrasses, plastic bullets, strip searches, a whole catalogue of oppression and repression that former Southern Foreign Minister — and vehement opponent of the IRA — Peter Barry summed up in the phrase "the nationalist nightmare". And as British solution after solution has failed to solve the problem, more and more nationalists have concluded that there is no solution within the Partition set-up; that, as Charles Haughey put it in a phrase that may return to haunt him, Northern Ireland is a "failed political entity".

On the question of the "men of violence" hijacking the civil rights movement, it was the attack on the nationalist ghettos in Belfast by the RUC, B Specials and armed loyalists in August 1969 that raised the demand for defence and created the Provisional IRA. And it was a failure by the civil rights leadership that it was not able to supply that defence in a way that would have subordinated physical force to political direction. And it was internment, Bloody Sunday and the capitulation to the loyalist stoppage in 1974 that made the "men of violence" a permanent part of the landscape. It was also the British government's intransigence during the 1981 hunger strike that gave the IRA and Sinn Féin a new lease of life, when they had been worn down by the attrition of the 1970s. If anyone transformed a non-violent movement into an armed uprising it was the Stormont government and its British backers.

Could it have been otherwise? Certainly I would have preferred the struggle to have been carried on by the methods of mass resistance: civil disobedience, protests, strikes, barricading areas etc. And I do not believe their potential had been exhausted before the struggle became almost exclusively a military one. But it was almost inevitable that when peaceful protest was put down by force many in the nationalist community would feel force could only be met by force, and there are many now prominent in politics North and South who agreed with them and supplied them with the arms with which to do it. There is no point in condemning the resort to force. All history teaches that oppression breeds violence. The way to end the violence is to end the oppression, and the professional condemners would be better occupied getting involved in the struggle against injustice in the North. But it cannot be denied, however, that the IRA's armed struggle has brought its share of horrors alongside those perpetrated by the British and the loyalists: Bloody Friday in Belfast in 1972, the Birmingham bombs, the White Cross bus killings in 1976, La Mon, Enniskillen. And the Ulsterisation of the war, pushing the UDR and the RUC into the front line instead of British troops, has had the effect, whatever the IRA's intentions, of making it appear a sectarian conflict.

IRA and Sinn Féin leaders now admit that there can be no military victory in this conflict. And the major moves by the British over the last 20 years — civil rights concessions, the suspension of Stormont, the Anglo-Irish Agreement — have all been made in response to mass political upsurges with substantial support in the South and elsewhere, not just to the IRA's military campaign. Rebuilding that sort of mass support, which stretches far beyond the ranks of republicans and small left-wing groups, is what is needed for another move forward. The IRA might now contribute more to building that support if they put their armed struggle on hold and concentrated on using the considerable political muscle Sinn Féin has developed since 1981. It could well be that as soon as any serious challenge to the sectarian state and to British control developed, the British would again use force to try to crush it, but at least it would be clear again just who was responsible for the violence.

Meanwhile, with disillusionment setting in over the Anglo-Irish Agreement even among SDLP supporters, with Sinn Féin showing greater political flexibility, and with the development of a new cadre of independent community activists in the North ready to take a stand on political issues, the potential is there for united campaigns on issues like discrimination and repression. Experience on issues like "supergrasses", the Birmingham Six and (in America) the MacBride Principles has shown that broad support can be built in the South, in the British Labour movement and in the US for campaigns on such issues. And since discrimination and repression are central to the existence of the Northern Ireland state and its British rulers have proved unwilling or unable to transform it, such campaigns would inevitably call in question the British presence and the existence of the state itself.

But what of the Protestant community in the North and what of the Southern state they would be asked to join when the British leave? One of the saddest aspects of racial or sectarian oppression is that it pits the poorest section of the advantaged group against the disadvantaged. And so it proved in Northern Ireland where the loyalist paramilitary groups have drawn their strongest support from working-class Protestants. Uniting the working class proved to be a lot harder than we had imagined in 1968 and at the nadir of the repression in the mid-'70s, when the nationalist population seemed to be fighting for its very survival, it almost disappeared from the agenda. But it has to be put back there. The Northern state will not be demolished without the support of at least a section of the Protestant working class and the acquiescence of others.

Developments in the South of Ireland over the last 20 years have not helped to win that support. The Southern state in the 1960s held little attraction for Northern Protestant workers; it was a confessional Catholic state run by a gombeen native bourgeoisie. The Catholic church had a special position in the constitution, divorce and contraceptives were banned, and the Catholic authorities were deferred to in a way that seemed to confirm Unionist claims that Home Rule meant Rome Rule. Moreover the working class was, if anything, worse off than in the North, where they benefited from the provisions of the British welfare state.

When Peoples Democracy held a march from Belfast to Dublin at Easter 1969, it was a rather naïve attempt to show that we did not aim at submerging the North in the existing Southern state, but at creating a new, non-sectarian, secular and radical society in the whole island. We aimed to link up with those forces, like the Dublin Housing Action Committee and trade union militants, who were already fighting for change in the South, but our approach was crude and simplistic. We thought the Southern political set-up would begin to crumble almost as quickly as the Northern one. We had a lot to learn about the dynamics of Southern society. One thing we learnt quickly enough, however, was how a movement that was lionised when it challenged the Unionist regime in the North could be vilified when it turned its attentions to the South.

The state established out of the victory of the conservative forces in the Irish civil war was more stable than we thought — though it did wobble badly after the attack on the Catholic ghettos in Belfast in August 1969, and after Bloody Sunday in January 1972 — and its rulers were a lot more ready to use repressive measures to prevent the Northern conflict spilling over into their territory than to change their own system to facilitate Irish unity. Twenty years later it has not changed much. The special position of the Catholic church in the constitution and the ban on contraceptives have gone, but sizeable majorities have voted to keep the ban on divorce and to write a new ban on abortion into the constitution, thus providing new ammunition for those out to whip up Northern Protestant fears. The South has also been badly hit by the world recession, with massive unemployment and emigration and with the major parties vying with each other in cutting public spending. At least in that North and South are now converging, but it is clearer than ever that if the Northern state is a failed political entity and the future lies in an all-Ireland state, then a major struggle is needed in the South as well to lay the foundations for a new socialist society transforming the two deformed states created by Partition.

The prospect for building links with the Protestant working class is not all that bleak. The last few years have seen the development of community groups in the North campaigning on housing and redevelopment and fighting cutbacks by the Thatcher government; of some trade union struggles involving mixed workforces, especially in the health services; of women's groups fighting their additional oppression within an oppressive society. All these have forged some links across the sectarian divide and have begun tentatively to take a stand on political/ security issues such as the use of "supergrasses" and plastic bullets, or the strip searching of women prisoners. The challenge is to link these groups and struggles with the fight against discrimination and repression of the nationalist community and bring home a realisation that the Northern state itself is inherently sectarian, repressive and irreformable.

In the South times have changed from the heady days when the Labour Party could confidently declare that "the '70s will be socialist", and the forces for change may seem to be at a low ebb. But there are some more hopeful stirrings. Trade unionists are growing disillusioned with the National Agreement and there is something of a revival of the left in the Labour Party. Sinn Féin have committed themselves to fight for change in the South as well as the North, there has been a major growth in radical community based politics, and women's groups, demoralised by the referenda defeats, are beginning to regroup and fight back. Again, the challenge is to weld these disparate forces into a united movement, convince them that so long as the Northern sore is left to fester its poison will continue to infect the body politic in the South, and win their support for building a new all-Ireland socialist society.

These are daunting tasks, but no more so than the vision that

73

inspired the initial revolt in the North of Ireland 20 years ago. There had been revolts in every decade of the history of the Northern state — proof in itself that it was rotten to the core— but none before now has lasted anything like as long or gone as near to the heart of the problem as that which began in 1968. And it has been given to no previous generation to take stock after 20 years of struggle under one form or another, reflect on its successes and its failures, and set out anew to finish the task.

A PEASANT IN THE
HALLS OF THE GREAT

Bernadette (Devlin) McAliskey was born on 23 April 1947 in Cookstown, County Tyrone, the third of six children. She was educated at primary level by the Sisters of Mercy, and thereafter at St Patrick's Academy, Dungannon, and Queen's University, Belfast. In April 1969 she was requested to leave Queen's and refused permission to sit her final exams for an honours degree in psychology as a direct consequence of her participation in the civil rights movement. This action was precipitated by the County Tyrone Education Authority, which symbolically revoked her scholarship. She has no formal qualifications.

She was MP for Mid-Ulster from April 1969 to February 1974, and married Michael McAliskey on 23 April 1973. She has three children, Róisín, Deirdre and Fintan. In 1979 she campaigned in the European Parliament elections in support of protesting republican prisoners. She and her husband survived an assassination attempt in January 1981 in which they were both seriously injured. She lives in Coalisland, County Tyrone, now aged 41, and "having outlived a great many people she loved".

There is a certain wry humour about knowing that you will be remembered in history for such Cuchullain-esque deeds as being the youngest whatever since whenever in the parliamentary saga and having abused the privilege by giving the British Home Secretary, an eminently forgettable Mr Maudling, a feeble-fisted belt on the jaw. For this I came into the world!

To dispose of the first myth briefly, for that is all it merits, the 21-year-old MP Bernadette Devlin entered the British House of Commons on 22 April 1969, and gained the somewhat less exciting age of 22 years the following day. I mention the point lest some aspiring record-breaker lose heart: there are 364 days by which this historic achievement can be surpassed, if you're into that sort of thing.

The "assault" on Reginald Maudling has more serious implications which I will deal with in sequence. Suffice at this point to recall with some sadness that as often as I am reminded of it, I am also asked, "What's this that was about?" The same question might indeed be asked about my entire "parliamentary career", as it is called, which came and went before I had reached an age when the average politician is only beginning to launch him- or herself on an unsuspecting electorate.

My parliamentary career was the result of neither desire, ambition, nor indeed effort on my part. In fact, I have been afflicted all my life by an inability to muster enough motivation even to comprehend ambition as a personal attribute. As a member of the student-based Peoples Democracy, I was one of a number of candidates in the 1969 elections to the Northern Ireland parliament at Stormont, in February of that year. Peoples Democracy contested the election against both the Unionist and Nationalist parties on a militant and radical programme. To the surprise of the pundits and, indeed, the Peoples Democracy itself, the group's success in the election was astounding and clearly demonstrated that the years of stagnation and quiet acceptance of "half a loaf" politics were at an end.

Those who choose to revise the history of the civil rights movement consistently argue that Peoples Democracy's Long March to Derry in January 1969 was unpopular, unwise, and started the derailment of the "non-violent, non-political, non-sectarian" civil rights bandwagon. To maintain that falsehood, the February 1969 elections have by and large been written out of history. Nonetheless, the reality remains that within weeks of the Long March Peoples Democracy made history, taking almost ten per cent of the votes in that election. Fergus Woods of Peoples Democracy came within less than a dozen votes of unseating the Nationalist MP for South Down, and I had secured almost every anti-Unionist vote in South Derry, where I stood against Major Chichester-Clark, later to become Prime Minister of Northern Ireland.

It was essentially Peoples Democracy's success in that election that set the stage for the Mid-Ulster by-election of April 1969, when I got elected to the Westminster parliament. The by-election was caused by the death of the Unionist MP Mr George Forrest. An opportunity therefore presented itself for the anti-Unionists to unite, assert their electoral majority in the constituency, and send to Westminster an ally for the West Belfast MP Gerry Fitt, then a member of the Republican Labour Party. It was easier said than done.

Mid-Ulster is historically a republican seat. It has never been wrested from the Unionists, despite its anti-Unionist majority, unless the candidate had the support of the republican movement. The history of electoral battles between republicans and nationalists in the area was a bitter one, where traditionally the "Hibernians" (conservative Catholic nationalists) had split the vote to unseat the successful republican. It was no secret that the Nationalist Party was grooming a young teacher, Austin Currie, for the Mid-Ulster seat. He was already a Stormont MP for East Tyrone, had a high profile in the civil rights movement, was politically articulate, capable, and seemed destined to go far. As a member of the Nationalist Party, however, he was totally unacceptable to the republicans, who maintained the abstentionist principle. Their candidate was Kevin Agnew, a County Derry solicitor and committed campaigner. He was a founder member of the Civil Rights Association, and his political credentials were at least as impressive as those of Austin Currie.

It was Patricia and Dr Con McCluskey, from the Dungannon-based Campaign for Social Justice, who devised the simple solution to the dilemma — let the people decide! They organized a series of meetings throughout the constituency, culminating in a delegate convention of the electorate to choose a candidate. Sadly, the contribution of Patricia McCluskey, in particular, in the early and mid-'60s, in documenting, highlighting and challenging the injustices of the Northern state, and laying the foundation for the civil rights movement has never been properly acknowledged. The popular approach of concentrating on the spectacular and on "public figures" in reporting events has denied and misrepresented the reality. By such means does history become distorted. In any event, the machinery was set in place, in the hope that public pressure would persuade the republicans to allow an "attendance" candidate to go forward — that candidate being Austin Currie.

As a direct result of Peoples Democracy's election success in February 1969, I was, without being aware of the fact, established as the "credible compromise", the second string on both the republican and nationalist bows. In the end, neither had any alternative except to postpone their own claims and temporarily hand Mid-Ulster over to the young woman from the university, with the clear intention on both sides of retrieving it at the earliest opportunity. Having been thus selected as the "Unity Candidate", I was virtually certain to be the MP for Mid-Ulster, and so it came to pass. I was elected with 33,648 votes to 29,437 for Mrs Forrest, the Unionist candidate.

What was expected of me politically was never stated by any of those who engineered my selection. I had, in fact, done all that I was asked or expected to do — I had beaten the Unionists. Now all that was required of me was "to be an MP". Nobody had objected to my writing my own political manifesto or campaigning on the basis of it. The only difference of opinion during the campaign was on the wisdom of campaigning for Protestant votes. I insisted on it and held meetings in Moneymore, Tobermore, Sion Mills — strongly Protestant villages — and everywhere in between. The return on the investment was minimal, but it was the principle that mattered! That I had political opinions of my own was never in doubt, nor was the realisation that I would express and advocate them. Everybody knew that. I was recognised as a militant, a radical, an outspoken young woman, but none of these things mattered for the moment. Nor did very many of the promoters of the Unity campaign look beyond the moment.

In retrospect, it is easy to see that because I was very young, female, radical and, they hoped, a temporary fixture, nobody considered it necessary to pay the slightest attention to what I thought. I, however, took my parliamentary position and my own opinions very seriously. I considered myself "a socialist of sorts". I was learning from experience and socialism made more sense to me than anything else I had heard. It still does. My own instincts and emerging political ideas led me to consider the alliances I could make outside the House of Commons of far greater value than those made inside it. I saw my potential allies in Britain as the trade unions, the British "left", the Irish in Britain, and the other oppressed minorities, with the result that when I was not in Westminster, for the very few occasions when Northern Ireland was allowed to be discussed, or not in the North itself, I was speaking throughout England, Scotland and Wales on the "Irish Question". Moreover, it did not seem to me that prejudice, poverty, discrimination, repression and racism were confined only to the North of Ireland. I could see them everywhere I spoke, and can still not comprehend the mentality that argues that I should have pretended not to see them, because it wasn't my business.

Thus ended the "honeymoon" between parliament, press, and the youngest MP since Pitt, almost as soon as it had begun. On the British front, my list of unforgiveable activities included supporting the dockers' strike, the Ford workers' strike at Dagenham, the Birmingham Indian Workers Association's campaign against racism, the rights of the travelling people, and my refusal to bow three times in deference to the wisdom of the British Labour Party leadership on these matters.

In parliament, I was a pain in the neck. There was a "convention" which did not allow any matters concerning Northern Ireland to be raised if they could be raised instead in the Stormont parliament. I refused to accept this and, having studied Erskine's *Parliamentary Practice* at some length, was given to jumping up under standing orders to relate the events taking place at home, when nobody wanted to hear. This unparliamentary behaviour was an embarrassment to Gerry Fitt, who had learned to behave himself, and to the Labour Party.

My most vivid memories of the hypocrisy of that place are three-fold. There was the time when John Hume and several thousand others had taken to sitting in the middle of the road. A British soldier had foolishly quoted the "Special Powers Act" as his authority for bodily removing Mr Hume and arresting him. This was a mistake! The Special Powers Act, a notorious piece of legislation, had one fundamental flaw. It read: "The Special Powers Act shall *not* apply to Her Majesty's Armed Forces ...". The late Bowes Egan, a Fermanagh-born law lecturer who had been one of the Peoples Democracy candidates in the February 1969 election, had been making this very point since the arrival of British soldiers on the streets in the North in August 1969. Hundreds, probably thousands of people had been unlawfully stopped, questioned, searched, arrested and imprisoned, interned, and had had their property invaded, ransacked and confiscated by the British soldiers. But these were not John Hume, and it was only when John Hume, by then a Stormont MP and already talent-spotted as the leading "moderate" in the civil rights movement, was so arrested that the Parliamentary Labour Party dug Bowes Egan's documented assertion out of the waste-paper basket and finally cried "foul play". The government could not deny it. It was there in black and white!

At the time, the attention of the British parliament was concentrated on the question of whether to increase the old age pension by £1.00. The decision had been taken in principle, but the snail-like pace of parliamentary procedure meant that by the time the £1.00 reached the pension books, the rising cost of living would have reduced its value to practically nothing. Reluctantly, the Labour Party accepted the slow workings of the parliamentary wheelbarrow, and were advocating a larger initial payment. However, at 3.30p.m. one day, in the middle of the pension debate, the appropriate Minister for Skullduggery came before the House and announced that the government wished as a matter of urgency to lay a new Bill before parliament, to deal with the embarrassing illegality of the soldiery in Northern Ireland.

The Bill was simple enough. It was to amend the law which said: "The Special Powers Act shall *not* apply", to read "*shall* apply, and shall be deemed always to have applied". This small word change effectively introduced retrospective legislation, contrary to international law — making laws for the past as well as for the present and the future. And it gave the British army powers which had previously applied only to the RUC and B Specials, and which had prevented Britain from fulfilling her international human rights obligations under the European Convention on Human Rights. Nonetheless, by 3.30p.m. the following day the Bill had passed through all the stages required in the House of Commons and the House of Lords and had been signed by the Queen. So much for law, democracy, and so much for the old age pension increase, which took almost six months to see the Queen's signature!

The ineffective whimpering of the Labour Party on the issue was the start of a pattern repeated over 20 years. They complained that the action of the government was illegal, undemocratic, draconian, a breach of civil liberties — and then did nothing to try to prevent it, since they considered that "in the interests of security" it ought to happen anyway. Without the agreement of the Parliamentary Labour Party not to impede the passage of the Bill, it could not have been rushed through the way it was.

When the Ulster Defence Regiment (UDR), a new locally-recruited part-time militia, was being set up that, too, required legislation at Westminster and, again, it was my argument that the legislation could effectively be stopped. The procedure was simple enough: we would talk it out of existence. This tactic, first developed by Charles Stewart Parnell in the late nineteenth century, had become a standard and effective weapon in the House of Commons. It required keeping up speeches from 3.30p.m. on one day to 3.30p.m. the next. The Parliamentary timetable then required that the proposed legislation be put back to the next term, when the procedure could be repeated. Our campaign started well enough, but when the press gallery emptied at 8.30p.m. Gerry Fitt, Paul Rose MP and the Campaign for Democracy in Ulster, which had 100 MPs as members, threw in the towel and went home. By 9a.m. the following morning, only Michael Foot MP and myself remained. We had been there all night, speaking in turn, while Bowes Egan, Eamonn McCann, Gery Lawless and a number of others frantically devised new material for speeches. We were not permitted to make the same point twice, we could not introduce irrelevant material, and we could not read speeches. But we kept going, until sheer exhaustion drove Michael Foot out of the debating chamber. I continued until I literally had no voice left and the Speaker called for the next person who wished to speak in the debate. There being nobody else, the debate was closed and the UDR established. All this time, sufficient members of parliament had been kept in the vicinity, in the event of a vote being called. Publicly, Gerry Fitt and the "Irish lobby" in the Labour Party were opposed to establishing the UDR. Privately, however, they were not prepared to prevent it happening.

People do not recall these events because they were never informed about them. They do, however, vividly recall the striking of the Home Secretary, although that is all many do remember, until it is pointed out that it happened in the aftermath of "Bloody Sunday" in January 1972, when 13 civilians were shot dead by the British army during a civil rights demonstration in Derry. I was part of Bloody Sunday, and it is one of the events of the past 20 years which I recall, like a slow-motion video, a nightmare in which I see myself from outside myself, and experience in seeing it again the depth of fear, confusion, anger and sheer helplessness I felt at the time.

Only those who have shared the experience can truly understand the feeling of latent power that is created when the powerless unite and congregate in their thousands to make one single voice of protest. On that Sunday, 30 January, we gathered 35,000 strong on the hill in the Creggan estate in Derry, overlooking the Bogside, to protest about the introduction of internment without trial. We flowed down that hill and we felt strong. Despite everything that had been inflicted upon us at that stage, we were still marching and singing. We knew that we would not be permitted into the walled city in the centre of Derry. We would march up to the barricade, protest at being stopped, and then swing right into the Bogside to hold our meeting.

There was an element of ritual to these marches. Our way was always blocked with the familiar barriers, the soldiers and RUC on one side, us on the other. The mutual exchange of stones would take place, but it was before the era of the "plastic bullet" and in order for the troops and RUC to get at us the barriers had to be removed. So there was time to run if we were attacked. And so it was that day. Those of us at the head of the march had already turned into the Bogside and reached the platform at Free Derry corner and the rest were making their way towards it.

I was standing on the platform when the first shots were fired. I assumed that the soldiers on the walls of the old city, overlooking the Bogside, were firing over our heads to frighten us. Looking down at 35,000 faces, I had just started to say: "Don't be afraid", when before my eyes I saw the 35,000 people literally fall to their knees as the firing continued. In the same instant I dived off and under the platform in one movement, still holding the mike. Years of tradition and upbringing kept the words: "Protect me in the hour of death" pounding in my head. Realising I still had the microphone, I started to speak, urging people to crawl away from the place without standing up.

When I finally looked at the open space, there were still a few people lying there. I thought they were too frightened to move. I spoke again and, as I did, the reality dawned on me. They were dead.

I got up and ran all the way to Nell McCafferty's house. It was over. The British army was everywhere. People were shouting in fear and anger, some of them crying. Others were searching for friends lost in the panic. From Nell's house I rang Altnagelvin hospital. I was an MP, so I could get information. There were dead and injured and I was given the names of people who might be best advised to come to the hospital, but I was told I should not tell them their son or brother was dead. Thirteen bodies in the morgue! Thirteen people slaughtered on their own streets for no reason other than to inflict terror and so put a stop to the non-violent civil rights movement.

I returned to Westminster where the Secretary of State was to make a statement on the shooting of unarmed civilians by paratroops.

Parliament has its rules, regulations and traditions. On every occasion where Ireland was concerned, parliament ignored these rules if they did not suit the undemocratic activity they were involved in or trying to conceal. So with Bloody Sunday. The tradition of the House of Commons is that when an incident or issue arises in which an MP has a declared involvement, or to which he/she was witness, then following the party leaders etc., that member has priority and will be recognised by the Speaker and called to speak on the matter early in the discussion. Not only was I not recognised and called to speak early, I was not called to speak at all.

I followed the rules of the House and got up on a point of order, to point out to the Speaker that I had not spoken and ask him not to close the discussion until I had been given the opportunity to speak. The Speaker immediately closed the debate. I followed the procedure again and on a point of order challenged the ruling and asked for the debate to continue. Finally I rose to make a point of censure on the Speaker for denying me my rights as an MP. During all this nobody in that cradle of democracy supported my right to speak except Frank McManus, MP for Fermanagh-South Tyrone, who had been elected, also as a Unity candidate and because of his involvement in the civil rights campaign, in the 1970 general election. The Speaker got to his feet, which in the ritual of the place demands that everybody else sits down and shuts up. He declared: "The Honourable member for Mid-Ulster has no rights in this House save those accorded to her by the Speaker", and moved to the next business.

When democracy is found wanting, it must be challenged, so at that point I got up and replied that the Home Secretary was "lieing through his teeth". This caused uproar and I was asked to withdraw the statement, but I was now angered to breaking point. Declaring that I had whatever rights I had it in my power to assert, I crossed the floor and struck the Home Secretary, Reginald Maudling. Consternation broke out, the sitting was abandoned, the shop closed down, and all the members of parliament who had sat silently, or opposed noisily as I tried to speak rediscovered their passionate commitment to the rules of the House. The British media, parliament and public were more upset by the fact that "violence" had occurred in parliament than that the British army had opened fire on a demonstration killing 13 people. It was a lesson in parliamentary democracy never to be forgotten.

The episode is recorded in Hansard with one word: "Disturbance", and the role of Frank McManus in my defence, both verbally and physically, is obliterated. Indeed, Frank McManus's period as an MP, his involvement and contribution to the ongoing struggle to be heard, to be listened to, to be believed, has essentially been written out of the history of the time. I do not believe this is accidental, or a reflection on his value. It is my honestly held, if subjective opinion that the deliberate misrepresentation of the political developments between 1969 and 1973 by those in a position to control the dissemination of information, the shaping of "public opinion" and the public analysis of the situation, could only have been done by selectively presenting certain facts, and drawing conclusions from them that only appeared to have any credibility if one ignored and denied the reality of the remaining contradictory evidence.

To explain that: the public portrayal of Bernadette Devlin, later McAliskey, is that of a remarkably articulate, talented and earnest young woman, who came to prominence in the "heady days" and fell from grace because she could not behave herself in a manner befitting her station, got "carried away", trotted around the globe, incited riots, alienated her supporters, failed to deliver the goods, and gave birth to a daughter outside the institution of marriage. All of that only makes sense if you forget that Frank McManus MP did not do any of these things, and yet he met the same fate as myself. This portrayal ignores the political realities. Following the "Battle of the Bogside" in August 1969, I had in fact been re-elected in June 1970, despite a feeble Hibernian attempt again to unseat a "republican".

The Battle of the Bogside occurred after the annual Apprentice Boys parade on 12 August, which brought thousands of loyalists from all over the North to Derry to flaunt their supremacy over the city's nationalist majority. This parade sparked off a pitched battle between the RUC and the people of the Bogside, which lasted for three days, spread to Belfast and many other nationalist areas of the North and ended with the British army on the streets of Northern Ireland.

Police attacks on the Bogside had been growing in frequency and ferocity since January 1969 and in preparation for what they reckoned was an inevitable assault on 12 August, a Citizens Defence Committee had been organized to prevent the loyalists, in or out of uniform, from gaining access to the Bogside that day. Barricades were erected and patrolled and preparations made to defend the area. The people of the Bogside had been unofficially confined to the ghetto for the day and various activities had been organized to keep them occupied. I was not a member of the Defence Committee, nor was I even a native of Derry. I just happened to be there, using the opportunity to record interviews for a programme with Derry activists like Eamonn McCann and Nell McCafferty.

When, after the march, the inevitable happened and the RUC tried to force their way into the Bogside, they were beaten off. But it then became obvious that, having resisted the attempted invasion, we would pay dearly for our impudence should we fail to keep the RUC out. We had little alternative but to battle on. It seemed as if every RUC man in the North was in Derry and then the B Specials, the entirely Protestant and loyalist part-time militia and forerunners of the Ulster Defence Regiment, were called out for service.

When the British army was put on the streets, it was not because Catholics or nationalists were under attack. It was because the Catholics under attack were fighting back and thereby destabilising the state. Eddie McAteer (leader of the old-style Nationalist Party in the Stormont parliament), John Hume and Paddy Doherty (a prominent community leader in Derry) then appeared in the Bogside ahead of the soldiers and declared that Northern Ireland was in a state of virtual collapse, the RUC were beaten and we were "on the way home". For disagreeing with this viewpoint I was virtually thrown out of Derry and was physically thrown off the platform at a public meeting that evening. For three days and nights I had fought and organized, encouraged and berated those around me, like everybody else who was part of the battle. Now the clean-shirted men asserted their authority as the Defence Committee.

As a result of the Battle of the Bogside, I was charged with and convicted of "riotous behaviour, incitement to riot, organizing a riot, and occasioning actual bodily harm to a police officer". Immediately after the result of the 1970 Westminster election was declared — when I was re-elected — I was sentenced to six months in Armagh jail. When I was in prison, John Hume, Gerry Fitt, Austin Currie, Paddy Devlin, Ivan Cooper and Paddy O'Hanlon, all MPs in the Stormont parliament, formed the SDLP, capitalising on the successes of the civil rights movement. They did so with as few original members as Ruadhrí O Bradaigh, Seán MacStiofáin and Dáithí O Conaill had when they formed Provisional Sinn Féin. The civil rights movement was not, therefore, taken over by Sinn Féin, as the establishment commentators now claim — rather it fragmented under the political strain of events into its natural components.

Frank McManus, myself, and almost every other elected "minority" representative at either Stormont or local council level were given what amounted to an ultimatum— either we joined the SDLP or at the next election they would contest our seats, split the vote, and remove us from office. And that is exactly what they did, under the slogan: "The SDLP is the elected voice of the 'minority'". In 1974 both Mid-Ulster and Fermanagh-South Tyrone were, in the time-honoured tradition of the Hibernians, handed back to the Unionist Party, when SDLP candidates were nominated against myself and Frank McManus without any hope of success for themselves, but simply in order to put us out. We had refused to join the new party and it was a political decision taken by the SDLP in the interests of promoting and strengthening the party.

There had also, of course, been the saga of my exploits in America immediately following the Battle of the Bogside, which had been noted down to be used in evidence against me in the eventual purge. I had been sent to the United States direct from Derry simply to get me out of the way. Because I totally refused to accept the presence of the British army as a welcome development, the respectable and the wise feared that I might encourage the people of the Bogside to keep the troops out, so they sent me to the United States to get me out of harm's way and because they thought I might actually be an advantage there. After all, it was generally believed that America was full of Irish people willing to give support and money and all you had to do was smile and take it off them.

I was not very long there until, like water, I found my own level. "My people" — the people who knew about oppression, discrimination, prejudice, poverty and the frustration and despair that they produce — were not Irish Americans. They were black, Puerto Rican, Chicano. And those who were supposed to be "my people", the Irish Americans who knew about English misrule and the Famine and supported the civil rights movement at home, and knew that Partition and England were the cause of the problem, looked and sounded to me like Orangemen. They said exactly the same things about blacks that the loyalists said about us at home.

In New York I was given the key to the city by the mayor, an honour not to be sneezed at. I gave it to the Black Panthers, a militant and militarist group of young black activists who at that time were the targets of a "shoot to kill" policy by the police. In Chicago I was escorted by the city police from the airport to the city hall to meet Mayor Daley. I refused to get out of the car: I would not be caught dead with Mayor Daley, notorious for ordering a brutal police assault on anti-Vietnam War demonstrators at the Democratic Party Convention in Chicago just 12 months before. In Detroit I refused to speak at a rally of several thousand people until the young black people who thronged outside the door were let in. And I added insult to injury by asking the young man who had been employed to sing John McCormack songs during the interval to join me in closing the meeting by singing "We Shall Overcome". He was black. In San Francisco I went to visit Angela Davis in jail. She was not only black but a communist. Irish America has taken 15 years to forgive me my trespasses, as they saw them. I had defied them in the cities they owned.

All this became part of the campaign against me by the respectable leaders of the "minority" at home. In short, I was deemed unfit to be a member of parliament because I would not confine my activities to the House of Commons, my politics to Ireland and my travels to London and Mid-Ulster. It is now totally accepted, of course, that John Hume and others should travel to Europe, America and elsewhere, and nowadays we are daily confronted with comparisons of our own situation in the North of Ireland with other areas of conflict. I confess that I derive most satisfaction now from the knowledge that the mayors of Chicago, San Francisco and Detroit are black, that the most outspoken candidate in defence of the Irish in the recent US

Presidential primaries, Jesse Jackson, is black and that almost 20 years ago my cardinal sin in the eyes of many Irish Americans, and Irish at home, was refusing to accommodate Irish-American prejudice against the black community in the United States.

I have always known what I thought, what I was doing and why I believed I was right. I still do and I content myself that there was a time in the history of the world when all "decent, civilised, respected and respectable people" — indeed the all-powerful "vast majority" — considered the world was flat. None of which had the slightest influence on the real shape of the world. It was round, but nobody knew — except Galileo, and they put him in jail for saying so!

ON THE STREETS IN DERRY AND LONDON

Geoffrey Bell was born in Belfast in 1947. He went to Derry in 1966 as a student at Magee University College; while there he became active in politics and joined the Derry Labour Party. He transferred to Trinity College, Dublin, in 1968, returning to Derry frequently. He graduated from Trinity in 1970 with an honours degree in history and politics and went to London in 1972 where he still lives and works. He is the author of *The Protestants of Ulster*, *Troublesome Business* and *The British in Ireland*. He has been politically active in the socialist and labour movement in Britain and is a leading campaigner there for British withdrawal from Ireland.

When I first went to live in Derry in 1966 it was a dying city. It had lots of charm, lots of wit, but it was stagnating and resigned to its fate. Or so it appeared. When I was back there, in February 1972 , attending the funerals of the victims of the British army massacre of Bloody Sunday, it was cold and it was raining. The city was in shock, its people in mourning, yet Derry had a different atmosphere from 1966. In the intervening years its people had fought back, and as a consequence the place had repossessed its self respect.

Remember that, because it is important to clarify what Derry and the North of Ireland were like before 1968. The sentimentality of the popular ballad "The Town I Loved So Well" is only appropriate to bar stools. It suggests that Derry was a wonderful, folksy place prior to the Troubles, when tragedy struck and turned everything to doom and gloom. It may indeed have been friendly and peaceful, just as the North of Ireland was largely crime-free, violence-free and orderly. But the peacefulness was imposed by defeats and the orderliness was there, not because people knew their places, but because they were kept in them. All that was changed by the events in Derry and elsewhere from 1968 to 1972 and to be a witness to them and, better still, to play a small part in them was an exhilarating experience, in which I gained a political education the like of which few contemporary European socialists have had the privilege of receiving.

When I went to live in London in 1972 it was also exhilarating. The Vietnam protests, the industrial and political battles over the Industrial Relations Act, then the miners and their victories over the Tory government. After which, when the Tories were driven from office in 1974, there was the optimism of the promise of new times. Being part of the "far left" was also enriching and, if trying to insert the issue of Ireland onto the political agenda was frustrating, there was still the sense of being part of a growing movement, confident of its own future. Or, again, so it appeared.

Living now in London in 1988, with its large areas of physical decay, its racism and brutality, the demoralisation of the left, and still the frustrations of trying to place Ireland on the political agenda is reminiscent of the sense of helplessness and hopelessness in Derry in 1966.

As to my part in the events of Derry 20 years ago, I could best describe it as being the megaphone carrier for Eamonn

McCann, the leading left-wing activist in the city at the time. Being a teenage Protestant from Belfast, even that was something of an honour. The key to it was membership of the Derry Labour Party. On paper and in theory that was the Derry branch of the Northern Ireland Labour Party (NILP), but for the left that link was something to be hidden. Whether that was because the NILP was such a moderate, unsocialist and ineffective party, or whether it was because the term "Northern Ireland" was not exactly a vote-getter in Derry's Bogside, I have never really known, but certainly "Derry Labour Party" had a much better ring to it. Along with that, membership allowed access to other agitational avenues, in particular the Young Socialists and the Derry Housing Action Committee; in fact, these two groups and the Derry Labour Party often shared a common membership. It was these people, together with a couple of young radical republicans, who were responsible for organizing the civil rights march of 5 October. Some 500 people marched that day, but the clash between the RUC and the demonstrators led to the education and organization of thousands more. That Derry was the spark that lit the fire was not so unexpected; the politics of those involved in organizing the march would always have allowed for that possibility.

In the North of Ireland generally the leadership of the civil rights organization was cautious and conservative. There was never much likelihood that they could control the movement they began with their support for the first civil rights march from Coalisland to Dungannon in August 1968. In Derry the traditional political opposition who could have been expected to seize the civil rights banner there, in particular the Nationalist Party, was demoralised and defeated. The decision of the Unionist government in 1964 not to site the University of Ulster in Derry was a body blow to the middle-class Catholic community and its constitutional nationalist politics. It was the poisonous icing on the unsavoury cake of unemployment, emigration and wretched housing which the Catholic community was forced to eat. The entire process of constitutional politics was morale-sapping anyway because of the gerrymandering of local government boundaries which denied the nationalist majority political control of the city. So it was not surprising that other forms of struggle, initiated by the less-restrained, emerged. To be blunt about it, Eamonn McCann, Dermie McClenaghan and those of us who tended to follow them, were troublemakers. The historical calamity for Unionism was that by trying to baton us off the streets on 5 October they allowed much, much more trouble to be made than would otherwise have been possible.

Even before the civil rights campaign got under way, in a by-election to the Stormont parliament in 1967, the Derry Labour Party fielded a radical English woman called Janet Wilcox whose husband was teaching in the city. To choose such a candidate was, in itself, to break from the political traditions of the North of Ireland, where candidates were usually identifiable representatives of their respective communities. And the conduct of the Wilcox campaign was also somewhat exceptional. As usual, the Unionist foe was targeted, especially the "Faceless Men" within the Unionist hierarchy in Derry who had privately lobbied against the city getting the university. But, even though it wasn't standing, battle was joined equally with the Nationalist Party — the "Green Tories" who were as upset as the Unionists by the radical socialist agitational politics emanating from the Derry Labour Party. Our "class not creed" rallying call also meant that we campaigned in Protestant areas, and, once, two of us went canvassing in one of the most famous, the Fountain. While we were there we experienced little overt hostility; the only awkward incident was when one middle-aged resident invited me into his house, pointed to a picture of King Billy on his wall and proclaimed, "That's the man I'm voting for." At the time that struck me more as banter than anything else.

Shortly afterwards, the car of my co-canvasser seized up. Later, sand in the petrol tank was diagnosed. It was a good while after that when someone wiser and older than ourselves gave us the obvious explanation: that the sand had been poured into the tank when we were in the Fountain. We were too naïve to have come to that conclusion ourselves. We were too optimistic that our socialism-for-all politics would ensure us a not too hostile reception amongst the Protestant working class. After all, we were out to save them as much as their Catholic counterparts.

It may be that those attitudes and politics were entirely exceptional among radicals of the civil rights movement, but that was not my experience. I had gone to Magee University College in Derry as a not untypical European '60s student, with idealism in the head and Dylan albums in the suitcase. Although a Protestant, I had had the good fortune not to have been brought up in an Orange home. As late as my early teens I would go to watch the annual Orange Order parade on the Twelfth of July and not have the faintest idea what the whole spectacle was about. When I did learn and when I read about the discrimination, the Special Powers Act and all the rest of the apparatus of the Orange state it was natural to conclude that it was unfair, even preposterous. Around the same time I developed a consciousness about being Irish, not from any political conviction but from ordinary things like listening to Irish folk music and feeling resentful against the English because their football team always managed to beat ours.

This development of Irish consciousness was exceptional. Although there were Protestants involved in the early days of the civil rights movement, when pacifism and reformism were in the ascendancy, there were not as many as later mythology has made out. Those who were active, like Ivan Cooper in Derry, were often awarded with more prominence than they might otherwise have received, simply because they were Protestants and because their participation was offered as proof of the non-sectarianism of the civil rights cause. However, from early '68 passive, reformist politics were to be severely tested, as were the Protestants who supported them, for the politics of the street were by then beckoning.

I left Derry in the summer of 1968 but returned for the march on 5 October, still feeling part of the movement that had called it. When I arrived in Derry I was disappointed at the small size of the march and felt slightly embarrassed because three Labour MPs had taken the trouble to come over from England to act as observers. I was as surprised as they must have been by what followed: the formal announcement by the RUC that the demonstration was banned; the police moving in behind us to prevent our retreat and then physically attacking us from the front with batons, blackthorn sticks, fists and finally water cannons. I suppose the collective memory of Derry Catholics had conditioned most of the marchers to expect such treatment, but for me it was as shocking as it was unexpected. I was too frightened at the time to appreciate the potential glory being bestowed on me for being there on that day.

Less than a year later, by August 1969, when large sections of the Catholic working class had started fighting for civil rights rather than just asking or marching for them, there were few Protestants on the streets in support. I was in Derry for the events of August '69 which ended with British troops marching back onto Irish streets. One morning, after a heavy night of street activity I returned to Dermie McClenaghan's house in the Bogside where

I was staying. His mother had two candles burning in the window, one for Dermie and one for me. Dermie shook his head and told his mother, "But Ma, Geoff's a Protestant". Mrs McClenaghan reacted with embarrassment, surprise and delight. The delight was symptomatic of the anti-sectarianism within that community; the surprise was all too justified given the growing sectarianism of the Protestant community. That sectarianism never appealed to me, because of my family background and because of the time I had spent in Derry and the people I had spent it with.

It may be that the anti-sectarianism of the civil rights movement in Derry was exceptional. Although its left wing did not enjoy majority support within the community, McCann and others still strongly influenced many of the activists, and the fact that this leadership always did stress their opposition to "Green Tories", and did genuinely want to build a movement which would attract the Protestant working class had an impact on the street-fighters, and did help the anti-sectarian cause. Even without that political leadership Derry might not have seen the ugly sectarianism which Belfast witnessed. There was an obvious difference between Belfast and Derry. In Belfast the Protestants were in the majority, thereby posing, and sadly proving, an ever present physical threat to the Catholic areas. In Derry Catholics were the majority, and because the civil rights cause was one not of dominance but of equality they never posed a physical threat to the Protestant community there. Of course, because the Protestants were in a minority, they had better sense than to try to invade the Catholic Bogside as loyalists had invaded Catholic areas of Belfast. It was the RUC which staged the incursions, which meant that when the Bogsiders of Derry fought, they always fought the forces of the state. It was, in that sense, a very "pure" uprising. And still we had dreams of an even purer one. I always got great applause for a song I made up to the tune of "Whiskey in the Jar". It began:

> As I was walking over
> The County Derry mountains,
> I saw the batons wielding,
> In the Bogside and the Fountain.

And it ended:
> So come all you working people
> Of each and all religions,
> Together we will march,
> And we'll form one brave contingent.

Even by the time of the Battle of the Bogside in August 1969 many remained oddly naïve, and not just about the prospect of working class togetherness. The momentous events began on 12 August with a clash between the RUC and some Derry "young hooligans", as they were called by their critics (and then, ironically, by themselves). The clashes took place during an Apprentice Boys march in the city, but it began as a just local skirmish. Then the entrance to the Bogside area was barricaded, with CS gas, bottles, and stones being thrown from the RUC side and petrol bombs, bottles and stones being hurled from ours. The crucial strategic point was the Rossville Flats, a huge tower block at the entrance to the Bogside. The local citizenry held that and by lobbing petrol bomb after petrol bomb onto the police below they were kept out of the Bogside for two nights and three days. The adrenalin flowed. I remember thinking just how serious the North of Ireland's political crisis had become, not just because of what was happening, but also because of the people to whom it was happening. Unlike other manifestations throughout the world in 1968, the uprising in the Bogside was as entirely proletarian as made no difference. I was one of the few students there. It was a natives' rebellion.

By the afternoon of 14 August the RUC were defeated, but those of us behind the barricades didn't know that then. It was the Bogsiders who felt they were under siege, under attack. And it appeared that way to others too. Jack Lynch on behalf of the 26 county government went on television and announced that he was moving the Irish army up to the Border. Which is how, when rumours of troops on the streets of Derry first reached those in the Bogside the initial assumption of many was that it was the Irish army coming in to rescue us, rather than, as it turned out, the British army coming in to relieve a defeated RUC. (If the Irish army did march into the Bogside today, the cynical assumption would probably be that it was they who were now coming to aid the RUC.)

Once the troops had arrived I was sent to Dublin to speak at a meeting there. I arrived with no accreditation except a spent CS gas cannister, but I informed the organizers of the meeting that I was there on behalf of the Derry Citizens Defense Committee. The meeting, held at the historic site of the Irish revolution, the General Post Office in O'Connell Street, was organized by what was to become Official Sinn Féin/IRA and later the Workers' Party. Their speakers had little to propose to the large crowd in terms of direct action. So, still holding to the "Tories Out, Orange and Green, North and South" line, I advised the spreading of the struggle into the 26 counties. In return I heard the demand thrown back at me: "Give us the guns, give us the guns."

After the meeting a section of the crowd went to an Irish army barracks where they demanded "the guns", but not for use against the Tories of the 26 counties. Although they were denied the weapons, the crowd then got into a couple of lorries and headed north. They never got past the Border.

Returning to Derry in 1972 for the funerals of the victims of Bloody Sunday was a different experience from any others I had there. I felt an outsider for the first time. Perhaps it was because I had not been back for a while, perhaps because I had not been on the Bloody Sunday demonstration, but I almost felt as if I was intruding on a private grief. Nevertheless, having lived in the city, having been privileged to be a small part of the struggle from 1966 to 1969, it was only natural that the murders on 31 January 1972 would hurt. It was a bloody, historic landmark. The killings were carried out by the British army. The attitude of the British government had gradually become clear from August 1969. Its continued endorsement of the Unionist government, its support for internment and the tortures inflicted on some of those interned had made it obvious that Britain was no longer a means to a solution, but part of the problem. Bloody Sunday and the subsequent cover-up confirmed this as no other event did. The Irish national question moved to the centre of the stage, where it has remained ever since.

Thus it was Derry which, from 1968 to 1972, played host to the three major events of those years which turned the historical pages: the 5 October civil rights march, the Battle of the Bogside, Bloody Sunday. Superficially, the first and third were victories for the "security forces": they did stop the demonstration in 1968, they did emerge from Bloody Sunday without a shot fired against them and 13, later 14 of the enemy dead. But, of course, neither of those brutalities were defeats for Derry's majority population. The political consequence of both sent Unionism and then Britain reeling.

It was good that it was Derry which saw these victories, just as it was good that the mass resistance of August 1969 occurred there. Because up until then the city had been part of Unionist folklore and a symbol of Unionist domination, from the siege of Derry in

1689 when the rebellious Catholic natives were kept at bay, through the election rigging of the Orange state which still kept the Catholic majority at bay and out of power, to the wretched social and economic conditions inflicted on that community; all of which was aimed at keeping those natives sullen and demoralised. If one memory above all others sums up, for me, how all this was turned around it was the sight of a group of the "young hooligans" manufacturing petrol bombs during the Battle of the Bogside, and what an elderly man said to them: "My God, if us lot 30 years ago had done what you lot are doing now, you wouldn't have to be doing it now."

It can be argued that the civil rights movement was a failure, as were some of the more ambitious aspirations of its left wing. The punishment handed out to those who fell foul of the state's political, security and judicial forces in the 1970s and '80s has been much worse than the few bruises handed out on 5 October. There has been no reduction in employment discrimination, and unemployment generally, for both Catholics and Protestants, is much worse. Most obvious of all, attempts to win sections of the Protestant working class to the anti-sectarian cause, to share a common purpose and a common politics with their Catholic sisters and brothers, have come to nought.

That particular failure was not through want of trying, but the efforts that were made, in Derry and elsewhere, from 1968 to 1972 showed that working-class unity will not be secured, no matter how much it is willed and worked for, while the iron law of Northern Ireland politics operates: the dominance of the national question. By the end of that period those of us who had gone through it had at least lost that much innocence. Others, outside observers had not. I remember a British socialist visiting a group of socialist republicans in Belfast in 1971 and advising us to go down to Harland and Wolfe and sell our newspapers there. "I tell you what, comrade!" came the reply, "You do it today and we'll do it tomorrow."

Twelve months after Bloody Sunday I was in London working with, or perhaps it would be more precise to say working on such comrades on the issue of Ireland. By and large I have been doing the same ever since. I have worked in the Irish solidarity campaign, the Troops Out Movement, the United Troops Out Movement, the Committee for British Withdrawal, the Bloody Sunday Commemoration Committee, the Labour Committee on Ireland and other variants of the Irish movement in Britain. There have been meetings in dingy rooms in dingy pubs in King's Cross, pickets at Downing Street, demonstrations hither and thither. Too often it has felt like swimming against a very strong tide of ignorance and apathy. Too often I have felt like echoing the sentiments of my fellow Belfast Protestant, Van Morrison:

> I'm going back,
> Going back,
> To my own ones

But that would be too self-indulgent. It is better to take the opportunity of the 20 years since 5 October 1968 and enquire into the state of the battle in Britain to take the Irish issue into the centre of British politics.

The withdrawal movement is the only one campaigning on the North of Ireland in Britain. There is no organization which puts out magazines supporting the Anglo-Irish accord. Far-right groupings like the National Front mouth their support for the Northern loyalists, but mount no campaigns for them. There is no sign of a repeat of 1912-14 when the British establishment organized and schemed to the point of rebellion against its own parliament in support of the Unionists. The formal link between the Conservative Party and the Unionist Party is gone. Within the rank and file of the Labour Party there is no significant organized opposition to the Labour Committee on Ireland which supports British withdrawal. At party conferences supporters of the Labour Party extending its organization to the North of Ireland appear, as do supporters of the Workers' Party, but neither have any base in the ranks of the party.

So, in terms of campaigning on the Irish issue, withdrawal has majority support, but despite that the successes of the withdrawal movement are few and far between. We "activists" have rarely numbered more than a few hundred, demonstrations have rarely attracted more than a few thousand and the movement has been riddled with splits, arguments and shabby manoeuvres.

There have been victories. The majority of local Labour Party branches have regularly voted in favour of British withdrawal at Labour Party conferences since 1983, and most probably do so for positive reasons rather than from the "Bring the boys home and let the mad Paddies fight it out" sentiment which probably accounts for opinion poll results in favour of withdrawal. A number of trade unions — the miners, the National Union of

Railwaymen and, most recently, the television technicians union ACTT — have also supported British withdrawal, as has the Labour Party Women's Conference and its London Regional Conference. Support for British withdrawal and concern over such issues as the Birmingham Six and the Guildford Four and the silencing of John Stalker are now part of the Labour left's "agenda" as nothing to do with Ireland ever was in the 1970s and early 1980s.

However, there has been no mass movement in Britain on the Irish issue, as there was or is on Vietnam, nuclear weapons or South Africa. Consequently, in terms of reactions within British society, governments from 1968 onwards have been able to get away with anything they wanted in Ireland. Part of my own political effort has been trying to figure out why this should be the case. An obvious and convenient target is the media with its abysmal standard of reporting and its deliberate misinformation. Another is the Prevention of Terrorism Act, which, at least in the 1970s, did help to silence the voice of protest against British policy in Ireland, especially within the Irish community in Britain. Some of the bombing activities of the IRA had the same effect. There are those who would go further and argue that it is the very nature and composition of the "struggle" in the North of Ireland which has done more than anything else to alienate support for that struggle.

The general explanation that it is all the Provos' fault might be valid if the reactions to the past and present Irish "Troubles" were notably different. Part of my own self-education and research has been to discover that this is not the case. As early as February 1844, when the British labour movement was in its infancy, H.M. Hyndman, one of the leaders of its left wing, insisted that the "real allies" of English workers were "the Irish people", but he added, "little as they [the English workers] realise it". This was to be all too obvious between 1916 and 1921 when the Irish struggle for independence reached its height. At the time the Independent Labour Party (ILP) had a membership of between 30,000 and 50,000 and had the largest individual membership of any left-wing party. In general it was sympathetic to Irish self-determination but its level of activity on the issue was a different story. Of 975 discussions or public meetings organized by its local branches in 1916, four were on Ireland; of 1,250 in 1920, thirty-nine; of 1,009 in 1921, twenty. In percentage terms, from 1916 to 1921 just over one per cent of the ILP branch activity was on Ireland.

Pondering why such antipathy to working on Ireland existed,

the nationalist author J.W. Good, writing in the Dublin magazine *Studies* in December 1920, had this to say:

> Why is it that in the main English Labour in its dealings with this country limits itself to abstract declarations of sympathy? Probe deeply in their minds, and one finds at every critical juncture the assumption that Irish democracy in so far as it pursues a different course from that which English democracy would map out, is recklessly abandoning the straight and narrow . . . in practice the trade unionist insists that the one thing necessary for (Ireland's) economic and political salvation is that we should sink everything else to become Labour men after his peculiar fashion.

This assessment holds true today for the British labour movement. When I first went to Britain and spoke at socialist meetings on Ireland I often lacked the confidence to give the audience anything other than what they wanted to hear. So I explained that what really was happening in the North of Ireland was to do with economic and social conditions, which at one level it was and is, but at another level it was much more than that. Anyway, that was often greeted as reassuring news by my listeners who, because they objected to nationalism within their own country, thought that the Irish variant must be equally unwelcome.

This desire to shape the Irish struggle into the image of their own is a never-ending idiosyncracy of many British socialists. In the mid-'70s the Socialist Workers Party (SWP) was successfully organizing a series of "Right to Work" marches. In a rare speech on Ireland, where by that time the Catholic community in the North was under daily attack from loyalist death squads and state forces, Tony Cliff, the SWP leader, proclaimed: "What the Irish workers need is a Right to Work march from Belfast to Dublin". Within the Labour Party the Militant group repeatedly argued that the solution was to have an Irish or Northern Irish Labour Party, based on the British model, and within it an Irish Militant tendency based, again, on the British example.

Others operated in a similar fashion within the withdrawal movement. Thus, if an organization decided that the best way to "build the party" was to work with students and recruit in the universities then this became the "way forward" for, say, the Troops Out Movement. Or, if it was judged vital to "enter" the Labour Party, then it was out of the Troops Out Movement and into an organization such as the Labour Committee on Ireland.

All this dawned on me rather slowly. In the early 1970s my

tactic was to look up Marx or Trotsky on Ireland and quote them to prove whatever point I was trying to make. The failure of one group I was in to take up Ireland as I thought it should prompted me to write a long document. I quoted Trotsky at the start — "The British socialist who fails to support the uprisings in Egypt, Ireland and India deserves to be branded with infamy, if not with a bullet" — and I even titled the piece, "If Not With a Bullet". As long as my thoughts were based on comrade Trotsky I was sure I would be appreciated. The leadership of the group expelled me two weeks later. Having recounted all of this it is only fair to add that the Trotskyist groups had a far better record on Ireland than any others. For instance, we used to jibe with much justification that the Communist Party of Great Britain — which declined to campaign for British withdrawal — was "all Great British and no communist".

It bears repeating that this rather gloomy view of trying to make Ireland an issue in Britain comes from an area — the British labour movement and the withdrawal current within it — which has been more productive than any other. On the other hand it would be to take too deterministic a view to say that nothing more could have or can be achieved. Too much energy and hope has been spent on trying to conjure up formulas of words which would "broaden the movement". It has been suggested that if only we were campaigning for say, "British withdrawal in stages over seven and two-thirds years, during which time British troops would be replaced by those from the United Nations one-third of which would wear green berets and the other third of which would wear orange ones", then the British public would have rallied to our banners as quickly as they buy the *Sun.* But the truth is that there is either support for British withdrawal more or less as soon as it can be achieved, or there is opposition to it. Attempts to build some kind of half-way house have been short-lived and dismal.

What is encouraging is that since the mid-'80s, when the Labour Party generally has moved to the right and when the left within it has shrunk, the agitation on Ireland has been exceptional in that it has gained wider acceptance within all sections of the party and stronger support within the left. The electoral victory of Bobby Sands in 1981 was probably the biggest single reason for this, but the fact that Tony Benn and Ken Livingstone have been prepared to campaign for British withdrawal and, equally importantly, to stand their ground when things got rough, has helped to educate those in the ranks of the party who listen to them and has given other, less prominent agitators on the Irish issue in the party the confidence to press ahead.

A remark made to me in 1986 by Peter Archer, the Labour Party's Shadow Northern Ireland Secretary, indicates a little of what has been achieved. I was debating with him on what Labour's Irish policy should be and he began his speech by saying, "Well, Geoffrey and I won't agree, but at least the Labour Party spokesperson on Northern Ireland is standing here discussing and debating the issue with him. That wouldn't have happened with most of my predecessors." Unfortunately, it is by no means likely to happen if any of his successors achieve government office. Nevertheless, it remains obvious that a major part of the strength of a future campaign on British withdrawal from Ireland will be located within the labour and socialist movements. Not exclusively, however, for since the early '80s there have been important developments elsewhere, specifically within the Irish community in Britain.

London now has three weekly newspapers exclusively aimed at the Irish community, there is an annual festival organized by the Federation of Irish Societies which can attract up to 100,000 people, there is another festival aimed at Irish youth which in its first year in 1987 attracted over 5,000. Indeed, hardly a week goes by in London which does not see some local Irish festival or other, often organized or sponsored by local government. There is also a "Sense of Ireland" month-long cultural festival and an annual Irish Book Fair in London, and at least half a dozen other Irish festivals, usually lasting at least a couple of days, elsewhere in Britain. There has also been a spectacular growth in Irish studies courses, in Irish language classes and in GAA activities. Many Labour councils in London now accept that the Irish are a distinctive ethnic minority and make provisions for them.

Part of the explanation for this is the increase in Irish immigration into London. Also, Ken Livingstone did a lot of pioneering work in many of the activities listed above. But there have also been important political and ideological developments within the Irish community, or at least sections of it. These amount to the rise of what could be called a "new consciousness" about being Irish and being Irish in Britain. Organizationally, this new consciousness is represented by the Irish in Britain Representation Group (IBRG) which was formed in the aftermath of the 1981 hunger strike and the ten deaths which followed. Although not a particularly large organization, the IBRG has been successful and effective in pressing the claims and rights of the Irish community as an ethnic minority. Its promotion of Irish assertiveness contrasts with the approach of the older and larger Federation of Irish Societies which is more conservative, Catholic and welfarist in orientation. The Federation's image of the Irish in Britain is of a community at peace with the host country; the IBRG argues that the Irish are discriminated against and need to organize and fight for their rights and for their sense of identity.

There is no doubt that the latter approach has struck a chord among significant sections of the Irish in Britain, whether or not they have heard of the IBRG. The growth of Irish immigration into Britain, especially working-class immigration, the poor conditions in which many immigrants live and the effect of the cases of the Birmingham Six and Guildford Four have produced a growing sense of Irish community solidarity. There is also an overtly political aspect to these developments. The Federation of Irish Societies would never dream of campaigning for British withdrawal from the North of Ireland, while the IBRG has a policy in support of it and has participated in many of the activities of the withdrawal movement.

There are historical precedents for this. Of all the many movements or campaigns on Ireland in Britain in the nineteenth and twentieth centuries the most impressive have been those rooted in the Irish in Britain. The Fenian Amnesty movement in the late 1860s and early 1870s is one example, although sections of the British left, particularly that represented by Marx and his followers, also participated. However, the Irish Self-Determination League (ISDL) of 1919-21 was, by its constitution, confined to Irish people in Britain or those of Irish descent. Established at the request of de Valera, it was heavily infiltrated by Scotland Yard, and was denounced as sinful by the Catholic church but despite that the ISDL was more successful than any organization before or since in politically organizing the Irish in Britain and in building a campaign on Ireland in Britain. There were tens of thousands of paid-up members, approximately 300 branches were established and it was capable of organizing simultaneous demonstrations of thousands strong in different cities on the same day at a couple of days' notice. Which is all the more impressive considering that it did not operate in Scotland where the Irish were organized politically on more overtly republican lines.

It would be a wild exaggeration to present the IBRG as an embryonic ISDL. Also, some of those involved in the growing Irish

Studies industry in Britain are anti-nationalist, anti-republican and take their intellectual lead from the "revisionist" academics in Ireland. But, accepting both these points, it remains the case that the growth and influence of the new consciousness among the Irish in Britain is reminiscent of a similar development at the time of the Irish War of Independence. It may be on a much smaller scale, but the gap could narrow in the years ahead. There are, after all, 500,000 southern Irish expected to emigrate to Britain over the next 25 years. If the most militant of them were to link up with the most militant of the labour movement then we "over there" may yet help to nudge Irish history along.

That would, personally speaking, be very welcome. The experience of trying to make Ireland an issue in British politics from 1972 has, in many ways, been the antithesis of my experience in Derry from 1966 to 1972. One was drama, exhilaration, the making of history, with elements of tragedy certainly, but above all witnessing the exercise of power by ordinary people. Trying to explain all that, argue its relevance and organize support for it in Britain has, by contrast, been frustrating, routine and the politics of the fringe. If this does not change it will be another problem for the Irish, in particular for those who work for a socialist republic there. But it would also prove a missed opportunity for their British counterparts. That point was made in July 1920 in Petrograd, at the Second Congress of the Communist International, held at the height of the still uncorrupted Russian revolution. The discussion was on the relationship between socialism, nationalism and the colonial revolution; it was attended by the leading revolutionary socialists throughout the world. A discussion took place on Ireland and the war taking place there. The English communists were admonished by the leaders of the International for not doing more on the issue. "The attitude of the English workers towards Ireland is the measure of the clarity of the communist mode of thought," they were told. When the English delegates objected that workers there would regard support for revolts against British imperialism as "treason", the reply came: "It must be said that the faster English workers learn to commit such treason, the better it will be for the revolutionary movement".

A wee bit of treason in England is long overdue.

A View From the South

Carol Coulter was born and grew up on a small farm near Tubbercurry, where her mother was the teacher in the local Church of Ireland school. She attended Alexandra school and college in Dublin, and then entered Trinity College, Dublin, in 1967 to study English.

She became involved in socialist politics in her first week in Trinity when she joined the Socialist Society, becoming its first chairman a year later. Through it she became involved with the Young Socialists and its parent organization, the Trotskyist League for a Workers' Republic, of which she was a member for many years. She was also active in the Students' Union, serving as chairman of the Graduate Students' Union for two years and contesting the presidency of the Union of Students in Ireland in 1975. She has been an active trade unionist since 1973, when she started teaching in Trinity. She has worked as a journalist since 1977 and now works in *The Irish Times*.

The events in Derry of 5 October 1968 came as a surprise — indeed, as a shock — to the thousands of young people in the South, especially Dublin, already radicalised by events far away and by their attempts to duplicate them at home.

In 1967-68 I was a first-year student in Trinity College Dublin. Although still the "Protestant" university, it was an ecumenical and multi-cultural institution compared with the tiny West of Ireland Protestant national school and the Protestant secondary school where I had hitherto received my education. Protestant and Catholic Irish students from North and South mingled with students from Britain, the United States and Africa. That year Dublin sparkled with excitement. The feeling, experienced by students and young people everywhere, that the world was going to change and that we were the generation that was going to bring this about, had taken root. All existing organizations were radicalised and new ones, many of them off-shoots of British left-wing groups, were formed. A major radicalising influence was the Vietnam war. Demonstrations against it attracted thousands of supporters, American officials came to the universities at their peril, and the Vietnamese flag was everywhere.

In May 1968 the weekly newspaper linked to the Union of Students in Ireland (USI), *Nusight*, became a monthly magazine, and for the next three years would give vivid and in-depth coverage and analysis of national and international affairs, sex, religion, culture ... and almost anything else that came to mind. The editorial in the first issue of the magazine expressed the self-confidence, or arrogance, felt by the generation it wrote for: "It is no cliché to say that the young men and women of this country have a duty to be bold, to lack fear and to stand up and be counted ... we readily admit we will advocate radical and fundamental change and we will do so with all the power and vehemence of our monstrous little voice." Its author was Michael Keating, now Progressive Democrat TD and the party's deputy leader.

The seeds of protest had been sown in the previous three or four years, which saw the advance of the civil rights movement in the United States and the growth everywhere of the anti-Vietnam war campaign. In 1967 the Union of Students in Ireland had participated in a "week of student solidarity with Vietnam". In that year, too, students in Berlin came onto the streets with their demands for student power and social change. At home the Labour Party decided never again to participate in a coalition government. In December 1967 Dr Noel Browne, Labour TD and veteran of a bitter clash with the Catholic bishops over his plans as Minister for Health for a free health service at the start of the '50s, addressed a meeting of several hundred students in University College Dublin (UCD) and brought them to their feet, applauding wildly, as he denounced the politics of the past 50 years, told them it was they who gave him hope for the future and promised them that "the '70s would be socialist". The universities branch of the Labour Party recruited by the hundred. The UCD authorities did not allow any left-wing or republican political societies to be formed, so there was little alternative to the Labour Party. In an attempt to circumvent this a Political Studies Society was formed. Its first auditor was Basil Miller and its first secretary Una Claffey, now a journalist with RTE's *Today Tonight.*

In Trinity the Students Representative Council, an officially recognised body far less colourful than the burgeoning student movement in UCD, adopted a programme seeking student participation in the decision-making process. The colour in Trinity was provided by the Internationalists, a group of about 30 Maoists whose all-out assault on all aspects of "imperialist culture" — particularly sex, drugs and rock-and-roll — deprived them of mass support. But in May 1968 they had their day of glory. The King and Queen of Belgium were visiting Ireland and this took in a visit to Trinity College. The Internationalists organized a demonstration against Belgian imperialism, supported by about 100 students, including the Trotskyist-inclined Socialist Society of which I was a member. The demonstration was led by a red banner proclaiming "Lumumba — tué par l'imperialisme Belgique". (Lumumba — killed by Belgian imperialism: Patrice Lumumba, leftist Premier of the former Belgian Congo, now Zaire, had been murdered by Belgian-backed secessionists after independence in 1961.) The police were called into the college, and there were scuffles, though no arrests. The whole incident would have been forgotten had not the *Evening Herald* blown it up into an outrage, and the next day the *Irish Independent* carried an editorial denouncing students in general and Trinity students in particular in the most vitriolic terms. This incensed the entire student body and many of the staff, and several thousand people marched to Independent House in Abbey Street to protest. The role of the

Independent Newspaper group in 1913, when it took the lead defending the lock-out of Dublin workers, was recalled, as was the anti-student coverage of the Axel Springer press group in Germany, whose vicious tirades had whipped up the climate of hysteria that had led to a murder bid on left-wing student leader Rudi Dutschke only a month before.

But these events were trivial in comparison with the other, more general campaigns in which radical students from both universities were involved. Those of us who were members of the Socialist Society, the Labour Party or the Political Studies Society were adamant that social change must involve the working class, and sought movements and organizations outside the college with which we could also be involved. The one which attracted most of us from these groups was the Young Socialists (YS), an organization mainly composed of working-class youth and led by a charismatic young electrical apprentice called Peter Graham. We all threw ourselves into a campaign led by the Dublin Housing Action Committee (DHAC). This had grown out of the activities of a city centre Sinn Féin advice centre and those who spearheaded the campaign were later to lead Official Sinn Féin, following the split with the Provisionals in 1970. It also involved two radical Jesuit priests, the Irish Workers' Party (the Southern wing of the Irish Communist Party), the Dublin Youth and Student Housing Action Group, the Young Socialists and the guiding spirit of the YS, a Trotskyist organization called the League for a Workers Republic.

The Dublin Housing Action Committee was formed in 1967 in response to the chronic housing shortage in Dublin which was the product of the policies pursued by Fianna Fáil in the '60s. These meant that the economic expansion produced by the inflow of foreign capital reduced emigration to a trickle, and the relative prosperity led to young people marrying earlier and starting families. However, there was no corresponding increase in house-building, and instead there was an unprecedented expansion in the building of office blocks in Dublin, involving the demolition of whole streets. Not only did this mean the destruction of Dublin's architectural heritage, but also the homes, albeit sub-standard ones, of hundreds of working-class families. The result was that thousands of people lived in over-crowded or sub-standard conditions. Numbers of them readily joined the campaign of the DHAC. This was matched by a wave of industrial militancy, to which the radical students also lent their support. Strikes like the bitter and long-drawn-out one at the EI plant in Shannon attracted carloads of students to its picket line.

The demands of the DHAC included the immediate declaration of a housing emergency, the ending of the building of "prestige" office blocks and the redirection of the capital and labour thus released into a house-building programme. The Committee picketed the monthly meetings of Dublin Corporation and supported homeless families moving into empty properties awaiting redevelopment. Squatting was a contentious issue in the campaign. Certain families, in despair, occupied empty Corporation houses. For other equally needy families still on the housing lists, this looked like queue-jumping. For the Corporation it was an added pressure, as they had to decide whether or not to evict the family. The DHAC was opposed to squatting in Corporation houses on the basis that it alienated the law-abiding on the housing list. The Young Socialists, and other more radical supporters of the DHAC, supported the squatters on the basis that squatting put far more pressure on the Corporation, and abiding by the law never got anyone anywhere. Meetings of the DHAC often resulted in fierce arguments on this issue. The radical activists also disagreed with the leadership of the DHAC on tactics during the pickets and demonstrations. At the time the reaction of the Fianna Fáil government to demonstrations was to break them up. The attitude of the Young Socialists and the student radicals — and the majority of the demonstrators — was defiance. There were regular mass pickets of Dublin City Hall and frequent demonstrations which usually ended in battles with the police.

However, the outstanding event of the first half of 1968 was the French General Strike. I still remember hearing the news. I was in O'Neill's pub in Suffolk Street with Basil Miller when another student burst in shouting: "There's a general strike in France!"

It was what we had been talking about all year, over endless cups of coffee in the Buttery, or in the cafes and pubs around College Street and St Stephen's Green. In opposition to the cynics and those from established parties and organizations, especially the then leadership of Sinn Féin who poured scorn on our views, we had maintained that students and workers could unite for a new world. Now here were workers supporting the demands of students for control over their own lives, for a new society in which equality and freedom would prevail, and doing so in opposition to the wishes of the leaders of the big party they had hitherto supported, the French Communist Party. This was indeed the beginning of a new world, which, for us, embraced Vietnam, where the Vietcong would win against American imperialism; Latin America, where the Bolivian revolution did not, we were sure, end with the death of Che Guevara in October 1967 and, of course, Eastern Europe, where the Czechoslovak students were showing that socialism and freedom were compatible.

Following the abatement of the events in France, those in Czechoslovakia were followed closely, and there were heated arguments between the radical students and members of the Young Socialists on the one hand and, on the other, those of the Irish Workers' Party and its youth wing, the Connolly Youth Movement, and Sinn Féin, all of whom oriented towards the views of the Soviet Union. With the exception of the supporters of the Soviet Union, the general view of the Czech events was summed up by Vincent Browne, then a radical young journalist, who wrote in *Nusight*: "Now the world ... knows that real socialism entails real freedom and real democracy". When the Russian invasion came in August 1968 it was a shock, but it only intensified the debate. It was widely felt that the Czechs would manage to hang on to their reforms.

So, in the summer of 1968 it was the activities in Vietnam, France, Chicago (the US Democratic Party Convention) and Czechoslovakia which preoccupied Dublin's radical youth. Another event, also abroad, worried some of them. In September, after years of deliberating, the Pope came to his conclusions about contraception, and published them in Humanae Vitae. All over Dublin people walked out of Mass when the encyclical was read out the following Sunday.

Like most Irish students, I worked over the summer. I saved some of the money to spend on a trip to Paris, hoping, even belatedly, to experience some of the revolutionary atmosphere at first hand. It was a sign of the times that, armed only with the addresses of members of left-wing organizations I had never met, I was sure of accommodation both in Paris and in London en route. And so it was that I learned of what happened on 5 October in Derry from a French newspaper in Paris. I was trapped there by my fixed-date ticket and lack of money, and spent a week impatiently kicking my heels until I could get back to Ireland.

In Ireland, the following week saw the formation of Peoples Democracy, the Queen's students marching and staging a sit-down in Belfast, Northern Ireland government representatives hurrying to talk to them, and the Paisleyites counter-demonstrating. In the South also there was a flurry of activity. Sinn Féin called a meeting whose platform was shared by the DHAC. At a march to the British embassy a week later a few petrol bombs were thrown. Among the major parties, too, there was intense activity. Fine Gael sent an inquiry team to Derry. The Taoiseach, Jack Lynch, made a speech in which he said: "Partition is the first and foremost root cause. And Partition arose out of British policy."

Meanwhile, his government had its own troubles. It lost, overwhelmingly, in its attempt to abolish proportional representation in a constitutional referendum. The wave of industrial unrest which had been going on all year reached a peak with a bus strike and an electricians' strike which hit the building industry. In the Young Socialists we saw a connection between the attitudes of the Fianna Fáil government to the workers, students and poor, and that of the Unionist government to the civil rights campaigners. At all demonstrations we shouted: "Tories Out, North and South!"

Although the movement in the North had developed very differently to that in the South, its leaders were not unknown to us. Most of the leaders of Peoples Democracy had been members of the Young Socialist Alliance in Belfast, loosely associated with the Young Socialists in Dublin. We had also looked with sympathy at Eamonn McCann's attempt to transform the Derry Labour Party, which paralleled our rather impatient attempts to do the same to branches of the Irish Labour Party. Another bond quickly became apparent. The leadership of the Northern Ireland Civil Rights Association (NICRA) resembled that of the DHAC. Both were strongly influenced by the Irish Workers' Party and its sister party in the North, the Communist Party of Northern Ireland. The leadership of Sinn Féin, who had come to prominence in the '60s, held views close to those of the Communist Party. We felt they were all too inclined to adopt moderate tactics and avoid outright confrontation with our respective governments.

The leaderships of these organizations saw the purpose of the civil rights campaign as achieving just that — civil rights — from the Unionist government based on the Stormont parliament they had always totally dominated. In the South they sought social reform, hoping, among other things, to bring Southern conditions and social services to an equal level with those in the North. Then, Sinn Féin explained, they would win national reunification and then — and only then — socialism. The Young Socialists and Peoples Democracy were not fully agreed, but they did agree on the need for social as well as political change in the North immediately. Seeking these changes was, for them, part of the general battle for socialism. Peoples Democracy argued that the issue in the North was not just job discrimination, but overall lack of jobs. The Young Socialists didn't think much could be obtained from either government in the way of reform. And we certainly did not want a united capitalist Ireland as a step along the road to a united socialist one.

In the North NICRA agreed to a government-proposed moratorium on demonstrations following the rash of protests after 5 October. So when Peoples Democracy announced that it was going to defy the moratorium and march from Belfast to Derry in January 1969 there was a number of student activists from the South who supported that decision and joined them. Among them was Basil Miller from UCD. The only student from Trinity who joined them was a class-mate of mine, the grandson of a Belfast Presbyterian minister and someone whose first-hand knowledge of it had led him to abhor Orangeism. After Burntollet, utterly intimidated by the violent attack on the marchers, he never joined another march.

Holding the mistaken opinion that the march was an empty symbolic gesture that did not mean very much, I did not join it, and was therefore among those who watched nightly on television as the demonstrators ran the gauntlet of loyalist abuse until they hit the organized assault at Burntollet. Until then Paisley and his supporters were largely figures of fun. Burntollet showed they were no laughing matter, and the marchers' triumphal entry into Derry showed that, by the people of Derry at least, their defiance of Unionist law was appreciated.

Meanwhile, radicalisation grew in the South as well. In January 1969 one of the leaders of the DHAC, Denis Dennehy, was jailed for squatting in a house in Mountjoy Square belonging to a property developer. He went on hunger strike, and a demonstration in his support attracted thousands of people, especially students, young workers and homeless families. We all decided to sit down on O'Connell Bridge (undoubtedly influenced by similar tactics in Belfast) and the crowd spilled up into D'Olier Street and Westmoreland Street, effectively choking the whole city centre. The police moved into the crowd to break up the demonstration, dragging some people away and hitting others with batons. I remember one of the most articulate of the Trinity student activists at the time, the chairman of the Socialist Society, Greg Murphy, standing in the middle of the crowd, with blood pouring from his nose into his red beard, shouting abuse at a Garda superintendent. Greg's late father had been an officer in the Gardaí as well, and the superintendent shouted back: "Shame on you! Why aren't you at home looking after your widowed mother?"

It was in UCD that there was the most faithful reflection of the international student movement. Students for Democratic Action (SDA), drawing inspiration from the SDS in the United States, was founded by a group of UCD students which included Basil Miller, John Feeney, Kevin Myers and Dave Grafton. In February 1969 a group of about 130 students, led by the SDA, occupied the UCD administration block, complaining about the lack of consultation in matters affecting them. They were joined by more and more students, including some supporters from Trinity like myself. Thirty-six hours later there were 4,000 there and at a mass meeting they unanimously supported the stance of the leaders on the need for change. A lecturer in economics mediated between the students and the authorities, and the latter made a number of concessions. The lecturer's name was Garret FitzGerald, and the reforms became known, somewhat to the disgust of their initiators, as the "Gentle Revolution". Some, but by no means all of those involved then threw their energies into support for the civil rights campaign in the North, and for the strikes and housing campaign continuing throughout Dublin.

Relations between Peoples Democracy and the Young Socialists and the Dublin radicals were not always cordial. We objected to their lack of structure and lack of clear (or, at least, clear to us) analysis or objectives. The Young Socialists saw a need to link the campaign against discrimination in the North to that against poverty in the South, and to proclaim as our objective a 32-county socialist republic. We felt Peoples Democracy was too inclined to limit its objectives to changes in the North, though it criticized society in the South. This was highlighted in incidents following Peoples Democracy's decision to march from Belfast to Dublin early in 1969, protesting at repressive legislation, including censorship and the bans on contraceptives and divorce in the South. The Young Socialists muttered angrily that they seemed to be missing the point about what the problem was, and maintained that it was necessary to highlight the fact that Britain was its root cause. As the Belfast march crossed the Border one of its leaders, Cyril Toman, brandished a copy of J.P. Donleavy's *The Ginger Man* in protest against censorship in the South. The book, though indeed once banned, was then freely available in Dublin bookshops. The welcome the march received as it arrived outside the Department of Justice in Dublin was lukewarm. An argument broke out immediately, with Peter Graham insisting that the demonstration should also go to the British embassy. The Young Socialists' banner led it off, and most of the marchers followed. However, the arguments continued at a social that night and ended in a punch-up between Basil Miller and Cyril Toman's brother Eddie.

While we in the Young Socialists and those who generally associated with us felt closest to the radical wing of the civil rights movement, the events in the North affected all political movements in the South. The big parties gave the movement as a whole nominal support, while Sinn Féin, South as well as North, saw in it the basis for a revival of their fortunes. For thousands of Labour Party members it was seen as part of the dawn of a new era in which "the '70s would be socialist". They identified with the role being played by the two Labour Parties in the North, the Northern Ireland Labour Party and Gerry Fitt's Republican Labour Party. In October 1968 they all came together in an all-Ireland Council of Labour and the Labour Party Conference the following January gave Paddy Devlin of the NILP and Gerry Fitt a tumultuous welcome. Fitt told the cheering delegates: "Next year we'll be here as delegates (of a united Labour Party)".

We in the Young Socialists had all been heavily involved in the Labour Party, helping to draw up its new policy documents during the preceding year. This conference saw the adoption by the Labour Party of the most radical policies it had had since the Second World War. It saw fierce battles between right and left wings on issues like workers' democracy in industry, education and contraception — battles won by the left. Many of these policies were proposed and spoken for by the younger members of the party, like me, who proposed the resolution on the legalisation of contraception. The party pledged itself to oppose all repressive legislation and heard party leader Brendan Corish promise that he would retire to the backbenches if it decided to enter a coalition again.

There were elections in both the North and South in the following year. The February 1969 election in the North saw a swing to Peoples Democracy and radical independent nationalists; among the Unionists the vote split between pro- and anti-O'Neill factions. In the June election in the South, Labour experienced a significant gain in votes, especially in Dublin, but few seats. This was blamed on Fianna Fáil's anti-communist scare tactics against the party.

After almost a year of campaigning, civil rights seemed no nearer in the North. Rioting began in Derry, and the uprising became acute on the night of 12 August. There were pogroms in Belfast. The South watched, horrified, as thousands of Catholics were driven from their homes by loyalists and their homes were burned. Many fled South. In Derry the B Specials ran amok, the barricades went up and "Free Derry" was born. The pressure on the Dublin government to do something was intense. On 13 August Jack Lynch made his now famous "We will not stand (idly) by" speech on television and moved the Irish army to the border, where they set up field hospitals.

There were nightly public meetings in O'Connell Street, addressed by leaders of Sinn Féin. Hundreds of young people were clamouring to go North to help defend their fellow-countrymen under siege. Sinn Féin actually brought a few lorry-loads as far as Dundalk, and then kept them there. The Young Socialists were urging people not to trust Sinn Féin and demanded that the government should open its arsenals to those prepared to defend the embattled nationalists. A lengthy supplement to the September issue of *Nusight* attempted to put the events in perspective. It dwelt on the differences now clearly emerging in the republican movement, which it described (in a rather oversimplified manner) as follows: "Thus while Sinn Féin tried to ensure that the South remained quiet and supported the militant postures of Fianna Fáil, the IRA claimed it was the provisional government of the entire country". This article was also critical of the way in which the question of Partition had been discussed in the South to date: "the Partition issue (while a valid objective) often proved a distraction for the really pressing issues of justice and freedom ... for it was frequently represented as an end in itself — quite divorced from other objectives". The magazine was a lone voice in the media in attempting a general analysis of the situation; by contrast, other publications reflected the general sense of panic brought about among all political figures by the events. For example, *Hibernia* praised the wisdom and statesmanship of the Labour Party in sending representatives to see the British Labour Party (then in government) in London, and in supporting Direct Rule by Britain as a solution to the crisis. It was critical of Lynch's initial belligerent response, and welcomed his more conciliatory remarks the following month. Above all, it expressed apprehension about the radicals in the civil rights movement.

The Dublin government was deeply shaken. According to *Nusight* "The tumultuous events in Northern Ireland caused the most serious crisis in Fianna Fáil since Jack Lynch became Taoiseach". The cabinet was more or less openly split between, on the one hand, those who wanted more aggressive action (to ward off the possibility that the leadership of the movement in the North would fall into more dangerous hands) and, on the other, Jack Lynch, who feared the consequences for the Southern state if it openly questioned the status of Northern Ireland — and, by implication, the whole Partition settlement — by a military intervention. Behind the scenes the events which were to lead to the Arms Trial in 1970 began to unfold.

1969 was the year in which the 1968 generation lost its political innocence. The illusions we had harboured just a year before that a wave of revolution was sweeping the world virtually unchecked, that we would thrust aside all reactionaries as we directed that wave, were shaken. The reactionaries had begun to fight back, starting with Burntollet. People were dying in the streets of Belfast and Derry, whole communities were being driven from their homes.

Abroad too, things were not so hopeful. The Gaullists were still in power in France, despite almost departing in the May events of the previous year. In Czechoslovakia, Jan Palach set fire to himself as reform after reform was dismantled, and the reformers were dismissed. It was going to be a longer and harder struggle than we had thought.

The next year, 1970, saw a counter-offensive from those afraid for the status quo. O'Neill had fallen in the North the previous year, to be replaced by Chichester-Clark, who was quickly followed by Brian Faulkner, the leader at the time of the hardliners in the Unionist Party. In the Fianna Fáil cabinet Jack Lynch moved against those he suspected of being involved in supplying arms to some of the insurgents in the North, and they were charged with illegally importing arms. Brendan Corish, leader of the Labour Party, said he was rethinking the "no coalition" position, and cited the Arms Trial and the "threat to the security of the state" it posed as one of the reasons.

The Young Socialists were heavily involved in the campaign in the Labour Party against coalition, and prepared to fight it at the forthcoming conference in December. They pledged to leave the party if a coalition policy was adopted. One of the leading Young Socialist members, Paddy Healy, ran for the Administrative Council of the Labour Party on this platform. He was elected at the December conference, but was expelled at the Council's first meeting.

This was the year, too, that the republican movement split. The long-brewing quarrel came to a head when the leadership established a majority for its policy of participating in elections in the South on the basis of taking seats in Leinster House and proposed this at the Ard Fheis. The IRA had already split on this issue, though its inability to defend the nationalist areas when under attack in August, due to the newly established non-militarist strategy of the leadership, fuelled the differences. Following the vote at the Sinn Féin Ard Fheis that year almost half the delegates walked out in the wake of Ruairí Ó Brádaigh and Dáithí Ó Conail to form Provisional Sinn Féin. There was already a Provisional Army Council. The Official republican movement continued to campaign for civil rights, though it also maintained defensive military activity for another two years. Its leadership was adamant, however, that the objective was reform in the North. The Provisional wing stressed that the root cause of the lack of civil rights was Partition and the British presence.

In the meantime the anti-coalition campaign in the Labour Party grew more intense. The Young Socialists hoped that Peoples Democracy and the Derry Labour Party would link up with the anti-coalition forces in the Labour Party, following an expected pro-coalition vote, to form a new all-Ireland movement which would carry on the fight for a 32-county socialist republic against all those we saw as compromisers and traitors. Eamonn McCann and the Peoples Democracy leaders did indeed come to Cork at the time of the Labour Party Conference and spoke at a meeting the night it opened, but they left Cork before the vote. The debate at the conference was heated, and for the Young Socialists the outcome was a foregone conclusion. We walked out, accompanied by Noel Browne and a number of his supporters, after the leadership won one of the preliminary votes on the issue. It was said later that the vote on the actual pro-coalition proposal would have been won by the anti-coalition forces had we stayed. Perhaps, and this would have been an important moral victory. But there was no doubt that Brendan Corish, Michael O'Leary, Brendan Halligan and others were intent on coalition and would have had it come hell or high water — or conference votes.

What was not so obvious at the time was that this marked the end of one set of possibilities for the radical movement of the late '60s. The many hundreds of young people who were involved in and around the Labour Party, most of them in the Young Socialists (which by now had branches in Sligo, Galway, Dundalk, Drogheda, Limerick and Cork as well as Dublin) had felt the Labour Party could provide some framework for combining the struggle for freedom and socialism with the struggle of their Northern colleagues against discrimination and the whole heritage of the Northern state. Those Northern colleagues were rather more sceptical about the party. In the event there was a lot of justification for their scepticism. Faced with the challenge to all the political institutions in Ireland represented by the events in Derry and their immediate aftermath, the leaders of the Labour Party gave up all pretence at seeking a radical transformation of society. It was the Arms Trial that convinced Brendan Corish to join in a coalition with Fine Gael. Clearly Fianna Fáil could not be trusted with the security of the state — the 26 county state, he implied. The Labour Party, founded before this state even existed, could no longer see beyond it.

The decision of the Labour Party to abandon its anti-coalition stance prompted a significant number to leave it, including the whole of the Young Socialists. They, the League for a Workers' Republic, ex-Labour Party members, Peoples Democracy, members of Derry Labour Party and other groups met in Dublin in 1971 and formed the Socialist Labour Alliance in an attempt to establish an all-Ireland political movement which would fight for socialism on an anti-imperialist basis. But it was already torn by differences between its component parts, all of which were more interested in establishing their own hegemony than in building the movement as an independent force, and it quickly disintegrated.

The other avenue the radical movement of 1968 could have followed was that offered by the republican movement. During the '60s it had begun to concern itself with social issues, though it never showed great enthusiasm for people organizing themselves independently of it on these issues. But this concern was combined with a re-evaluation of traditional republican thinking on the two Irish states. The leadership of the movement was steadily advancing towards a perspective of reforming them both. The corollary of this was to abandon, and eventually oppose, those who challenged the basis on which these states existed — Partition — and who contested that settlement. During the late '60s the claim of the republican movement that the Southern government implemented political and economic policies in line with the needs of British and American imperialism found a ready audience. But its leaders made no connection between this and the explosion in the North. On the contrary, those events deepened the polarisation between those who sought economic and social reform and those who mistrusted any diversion from their primary objective — to challenge Partition. The resulting split in 1970 posed the 1968 generation with an artificial choice between those seeking social change and those seeking an end to the Unionist state and all that went with it.

From 1970 on a process of dispersal of those radical forces began. The Internationalists disappeared, though their inheritors lived on in the form of the minuscule Communist Party of Ireland (Marxist Leninist). The Trotskyists of the Young Socialists/League for a Workers' Republic split once in 1970 and then a second time in 1971, the dissidents on both occasions inspired by international Trotskyist groupings. Peter Graham, the most outstanding Young Socialist leader, was mysteriously shot dead in a friend's flat in Dublin in 1971, and some of the other more prominent leaders dropped out of political activity over the next few years.

Still others from that generation turned their attention to specific issues. Of these the most important was the women's movement, which grew out of the mobilisation of the '60s. Campaigning initially for contraception and equal pay, it was the only movement of the early '70s to retain the dynamism of the '60s. It fed into the political parties and trade unions, creating an atmosphere favourable to the introduction of a body of legislation improving women's rights in employment and in control over their fertility. But its energy was drained, and its members dispersed, many of them into organizations produced by the reforms themselves. The limits of these reforms while the 26 county state, with its inbuilt clerical domination, remained intact, would become clear in the 1983 and 1986 referenda.

Other "veterans" of 1968 became, like me, trade union

activists. But the trade union movement offered stony ground for the ideals of 1968. Its structures were based on ensuring that the problems faced by the most oppressed members of the Irish working class, the Northern nationalists, would never get onto its agenda. The division between social and economic problems on the one hand, and broader political issues on the other, was maintained here too despite the efforts of some of us to oppose it. This division was breached, of course, in 1972, in the aftermath of Bloody Sunday, which provoked the biggest wave of demonstrations and strikes in the South seen since the Second World War. The trade unions officially sanctioned stoppages and demonstrations which culminated in the burning of the British embassy — but usually they sanctioned them only after their members had joined them anyway. This spontaneous expression of opposition to British policy in the North contributed substantially towards the abolition of Stormont.

It also terrified all the establishment politicians in the South and their ideological hangers-on, who began to try to put the genie back in the bottle. Consequently, the '70s saw an ideological offensive against Irish nationalism which sought to portray it as the expression of a desire on the part of Fianna Fáil and elements of the Catholic church to annexe the North. The fact that those who had opposed the policies of Britain and the Unionist government in the late '60s had clearly had nothing whatsoever to do with any establishment politicians was forgotten, as was the fact that they saw the necessity for a transformation of the whole of Irish society.

I think we were right in 1968 and 1969 to feel that these two states, both maimed at birth, had nothing to offer our generation. The proof is there today — almost everything about the North is worse than it was before, with the steady toll of deaths and teeming jails cancelling out any minor improvements in housing and legal rights for nationalists. In the South the moderation of the housing crisis, the reforms in the laws on contraception and women's rights at work, the real wage rises of the '70s, pale into insignificance beside all the evidence that as an economy the Southern state is a "failed entity", unable to provide employment for its tiny population. The two referenda, the resurgence of censorship, the structure of its education and health services, show that it is also far from being a genuinely democratic republic free from the domination of the Catholic church. At a political level, the virtual unanimity of the major parties in the Dáil shows how difficult it is for the dispossessed in the state to find an expression there.

Those of our generation still involved in radical politics could do worse than reach into our memories to reawaken the mistrust of established politicians and the faith in the thrust towards the total transformation of society we felt in 1968, and find a way to give them a more organized, thoughtful and coherent expression today. The problems our generation faced at the end of the '60s, which we tried to solve through large-scale social action in both parts of the country, still exist today. They can still be solved only through the methods we advocated then.

FROM CIVIL RIGHTS
TO WOMEN'S RIGHTS

Margaret Ward has lived in Belfast for most of her life. She attended convent school and then Queen's University, Belfast. She was also a Research Fellow at the Institute of Irish Studies at Queen's. A student member of Peoples Democracy, she has been a feminist campaigner since the early '70s and was a founder member of the Socialist Women's Group, the Belfast Women's Collective and the Northern Ireland Abortion Campaign. From 1984 to '86 she was development officer for women's activities with the Community Services Department of Belfast City Council, during which time she helped to establish *Women's News* as a forum for communication for Irishwomen.

She is the author of *Unmanageable Revolutionaries: women and Irish nationalism,* as well as numerous articles on historical and contemporary issues affecting women in Ireland. She now lives in Bristol with Paddy Hillyard and their children Fintan and Maeve, and she is completing a biographical study of Maud Gonne for a series to be published by Pandora.

In 1968 I was a sixth form convent schoolgirl living in Belfast. My father, who came from Dublin, was working as Recruiting Officer for the British army — which was not as great a contrast with his childhood as one might expect since he (and his mother) had previously been members of the Blueshirts, Ireland's home-grown fascist movement. My mother, on the other hand, came from Mayo and her brother had been in the IRA. One of mother's childhood memories was of hiding in ditches while the Black and Tans rampaged through her village. Although I often asked her about those times, my confused nationalist sympathies were based on the vaguest of historical understandings and certainly did not extend to any awareness of the nature of the Northern state. When we had first arrived in Belfast, seven years previously, we had lived at the top of the Crumlin Road and I couldn't understand why, every time I walked home from school, I was confronted by a gauntlet of thumps and kicks. My convent uniform was anathema to the young bloods of Everton school (the local Protestant school); ten years later, when school finished each day, army patrols would have to be used to separate out the different sectarian groupings.

Our geography teacher was a fervent republican (as I finally realised, many years later, when I saw her in the colour party at Maire Drumm's funeral)[1], and during the course of the Stormont election she conducted a secret ballot in her classroom. After some thought I marked it "Unionist" in the completely erroneous belief that I was voting for a United Ireland. Thirty-odd pieces of paper with "nationalist" were opened and counted. When my offending bit of paper was opened Miss McIlroy went apoplectic. That was my first political lesson. The following year the same teacher took us on a day trip to Dublin. We stamped our feet at the Boyne and choked back the tears as we were guided round the cells of Kilmainham Jail. At the GPO we flocked round the statue of Cuchulainn and listened reverently to the story of noble Patrick Pearse and his comrades. From that moment, for many of the fifth formers, Jesus was displaced as chief hero and martyr. Romantic nationalism became more important than religion. Both were emotional, typically adolescent, and had equally little contact with the real needs of people.

1968 — the year of the invasion of Czechoslovakia, the Paris

1. Maire Drumm was a leading member of Provisional Sinn Féin who was shot dead by loyalists in 1976.

May, of student revolt all over the world. The year of 'A' levels, of lost virginity, the start of a process of separation from family influences. And, of course, it was also the start of the civil rights movement and the challenge to Unionist domination. The summer of 1968 was the first I spent in Belfast. Every other year I had escaped to Mayo but now I was almost an adult and had a job as a hospital orderly. Working over the Twelfth of July was fine by me as it meant double money but after work, as I walked home from the Falls Road to the middle-class Antrim Road through streets full of litter and empty bottles, I remember pondering on what had been happening while I polished bed pans. At home the topic of Orangeism had always been avoided — as unsuitable a subject of conversation as sex or religious doubts. Such carefully fostered ignorance, like childhood itself, was soon to end. At the beginning of October I sat in the Club bar with my student boyfriend and his friends while they debated whether or not to go to Derry to join a civil rights march. I had never been to Derry in my life and couldn't imagine going all that way for a march when all I had experienced were the annual Corpus Christi processions. But on 5 October I saw my cousin being attacked by the RUC while I sat at home watching coverage of the march on television. It was unbelievable, it was impossible. What were the police doing? Why?

Four days later, students from Queen's University decided to march to the City Hall to protest against the brutality of the police in Derry. I decided, along with many of my classmates, to join in. We were supposed to be on a religious retreat at school — days of silence and prayers — but decided it was far more important (and more fun) to show solidarity with the civil rights marchers. Not wanting to look like a schoolgirl in front of university students, I borrowed my sister's big black hat. When the police stood in a phalanx blocking our route so that we had to sit down in Linenhall Street for three hours the hat came in very useful: a collection was made to buy sweets to pass the time and relieve the tedium of this particular non-violent protest. As we sat down, someone placed a "Smash Stormount" placard in my hand. At that time I don't think I had a clear idea of what Stormont was and it was debatable whether I could have spelled it properly myself. The Unionist paper, the *News Letter*, of course had no such difficulty. The next day a photo of my group appeared in it as evidence of student illiteracy and disloyalty, and those of us who had pretended to be on the retreat had some explaining to do.

The indignation felt by us all as Paisleyite supporters, backed up by an armed police force, denied us the right to walk peaceably through the streets of Belfast, led that day to the formation of Peoples Democracy. It was open to everyone to participate, students and non-students; in theory all were equal. But in an arena of hundreds, those who were young, inarticulate, politically naïve, sat quietly and listened. My boyfriend was elected to the so-called "faceless committee" of ten who were to administer the decisions made by the general meeting. I didn't see much of him during this time but when I did I got the inside story on everything. It was a vicarious existence — unable to participate fully myself but feeling as though I was — which is common to so many women who live their lives through their boyfriends or husbands.

A month or so after Peoples Democracy was formed an offshoot designed to give a role to younger activists — the Young Democrats — was launched. We met in a small dark room at the top of a rickety staircase in May Street. No one was too clear as to what our role should be, and I remember many meetings spent waiting for an "elder" from the university to come and advise us. One such, who did regularly attend our meetings, is now a senior social worker in Belfast and what the Young Democrats did was largely an extension of his preoccupations. Just before Christmas a family from the Falls had a fire which destroyed their house. Five of us from the Young Democrats spent the day before Christmas Eve in the pouring rain, collecting £30 for the children. The following day we bought them their presents and took them to Father Christmas. But being a more politicised version of the Catholic charitable agency, the Legion of Mary, was not going to further the revolution. We were all too well aware that the real excitement lay up University Road with the deliberations of Peoples Democracy. By mid-January the youth wing had been dissolved. It could have been invaluable in helping to educate those of us desperate for political knowledge, but in the excitement of those times I don't think anyone thought much about the needs of the individual. We fought on behalf of the Catholic population or for the working class; everything was subsumed into the struggle for such basic civil rights as the local government vote and the fair allocation of houses and jobs.

As I began to attend weekly Peoples Democracy meetings, relations with my father deteriorated. His power, as breadwinner, to determine what other members of the family did became increasingly evident. It was a tense and unhappy time. The officer in charge of the RUC Riot Squad was a close friend of my father and I found him as obnoxious in a social context as I did when he was on the streets directing his men to beat up students. When I heard that Bernadette Devlin had volunteered to sign the official form giving notice to the RUC for a march because she was an orphan and had nothing to lose, I envied her and longed to be a student with some measure of financial independence.

In all important respects, at that stage, men determined my life. Although I was surrounded by women at school their words reflected the values of patriarchal society and their determination to quell any hint of non-conformity led to my growing isolation from the school. I was refused permission to debate religion in our hard-won debating society in case I adversely affected the religious beliefs of the junior members of the school, and the nuns began to give me Catholic Truth Society leaflets on Connolly and on socialism in an attempt to curb my enthusiastic agnosticism. In the genteel atmosphere of the middle-class convent school, dissent was not encouraged. Although the nuns obviously resented the inequitable distribution of financial aid between themselves and the state schools, their entire philosophy was centered around trusting to the bishops and the power of prayer, with perhaps the odd word in the ear of a favourite nationalist politician. That attitude extended to the position of Catholics in the 6 counties and marching for civil rights was considered to be, at best, unladylike and possibly even sinful, given the presence of all those Protestant boys. Going to university was viewed with great suspicion by the nuns: it would mean mixing with boys and with Protestants. The worst catastrophe of all would be to meet a Protestant boy. In order to dissuade us, we were forced to attend an interview at St Mary's Teacher Training College which was run by the same order of nuns. I informed the panel that I had no intention of becoming a teacher and was determined to go to university, but they persisted in accepting me. I think the acceptance rate was in inverse proportion to our suitability, a way of keeping the rebels in the fold. Teaching was one of the few suitable occupations for women because the short day and long holidays meant (or so said the nuns) that we would be able to devote time to our children. And, of course, given the sectarian composition of schools in Northern Ireland, we would be working in an entirely Catholic atmosphere.

I spoke passionately in favour of black power at school debates, but it never occured to me then that as a Catholic and as a woman, I too lacked many basic human rights. The major political influence on civil rights marchers was the example of the black freedom movement in America; it was this, more than student protest, that Catholics related to. Or at least, those Catholics who had experienced the institutionalised discrimination at the heart of the Northern state. As a middle-class Catholic I knew I hadn't suffered the conditions of blacks in the southern states of the USA. I was shielded too from the brutal realities of Unionist rule and the existence of Catholic ghettos. I wanted socialism, but Connolly's *Labour in Irish History* was the only socialist book I had ever read. I had certainly never seen his writings on women, nor had many other people in those days before our history as women began to be reclaimed by activists and academics. Thousands of us shouted "One man, one vote" with great conviction around the streets of the North, and none of us queried whether this had any direct relevance to women. Peoples Democracy attempted to radicalise the civil rights programme by including the demands "one man, one job" and "one family, one house", and although I had a subconscious feeling that this really had very little to do with me, the fact that I was a woman and not a man never came to mind as an explanation. Such was the marginal position of women at that time. It is ironic that during the tenth anniversary commemoration of the Burntollet march, one young man began to chant "One person, one vote", only to be told that in the interests of historical accuracy there would have to be some alteration!

Peoples Democracy's attempt to appeal to the Protestant working class was, by early 1970, centred around supporting a housing campaign that had developed in many of the Belfast estates as a response to huge rent increases. A leaflet telling tenants of their rights and grant entitlements was prepared and 15,000 were distributed throughout Belfast. There were not many volunteers for leafletting Protestant areas and in general it was the younger and more naïve of us who, with hearts beating fast, dropped our leaflets through each door in the rows of small terraced houses and walked through what seemed to be lines of curious faces. Although I had lived in north Belfast for eight years this was the first time I had seen the reality that lay behind the Crumlin and Antrim Roads. Protestant privilege was a sad, shabby thing, but the sectarian divide remained.

surprising that no one at this time thought of women's liberation.

For a long time I rejected the idea that feminism could be progressive. By now steeped in marxist classics, I felt the formation of women's groups to be petty bourgeois and a diversion from class struggle. But as militarism became the dominant form of political struggle, there was little room for any politics that wasn't directly related to the war. And in the meantime women were also suffering discrimination and were denied — despite the contentious union with Britain — the legal reforms that had been won by British women. Women were also being battered and raped and there were no agencies to shelter them, no one to point out that battering and rape related to women's oppressed status within society, no one to campaign for refuges that would not be mere charitable agencies but would be informed by a philosophy of self-help and a belief in the validity of each woman's experience, no one to challenge the deep-rooted sexist attitudes that kept Irish women amongst the most disadvantaged in Europe. As a graduate student half-heartedly pursuing my researches on Connolly (a topic suggested by my male tutor) I was suddenly made aware of the invisibility of women from history and I finally realised that the explanation for this was linked to women's subordinate status in contemporary society. It was impossible to campaign for women without also uncovering the legacy of their past struggles: the personal was political and, in my life at least, both finally came together.

In the changed conditions of the mid-'70s the new layer of women activists were not students but the wives, mothers and sisters of those interned and imprisoned. They were fighting, not for themselves but for their families and for the return to a family life that had been disrupted by the forcible taking away of their menfolk. But in the process of becoming political actors and in the day-to-day struggle of living without the support of their men, these women began to find a strength and confidence within themselves that they hadn't dreamed of. Once feminists in the North did begin to organize, their major task would be to make links with those women and to attempt the development of a dialogue that could for the first time link the demand for national liberation with that of women's liberation.

It was impossible to remain within the privileged walls of the university while women suffered economic deprivation and endured the hardships imposed by a rapidly escalating war. At the beginning, organized feminism was confined to the two universities of Belfast and Coleraine and in both cases women deliberately set out to make contact with women from outside, to learn what the real issues were and to begin to formulate a set of demands that would at long last put the needs of women onto the political agenda. This is not the place to give a detailed history of feminist groups and their achievements[2] and I don't pretend to be a neutral commentator. I was a founder member of various groups: the Queen's (University) Women's Group, the Northern Ireland Women's Rights Movement, the Socialist Women's Group and the Belfast Women's Collective, amongst others. There have been numerous splits and disagreements from the beginning, but I firmly believe that out of the turmoil of the past 20 years the women's movement in its many different guises can point to a substantial and enduring body of achievement. Hard-won legal changes have helped alleviate the worst injustices, while the existence of numerous refuges, crisis centres and women's centres around the country, in addition to the various informal networks which link women from different geographical areas, ensure that women's voices are heard in many different spheres as women develop the capacity to campaign effectively on many different levels.

The uneasy relationship between those who concentrate their energies upon changing the position of women from within the perspective of the existing constitutional framework and those who argue that such changes are meaningless while the British occupation of Ireland continues has led to a polarisation that has held back the creation of a genuinely autonomous movement. But while those two views have tended to dominate, another small section of women has, from time to time, attempted to argue for the possibility of creating a movement that could fight for all women's demands while maintaining an anti-imperialist perspective independent of any political organization. In particular, the cult of militarism, which has been an integral part of so much of Irish resistance to oppression, has been heavily criticised by feminists for its emphasis on violence and implicit denial of mass political action.

The period of the Armagh women prisoners' campaign for

2. For readers interested in a more detailed narrative of the history of feminism in the North, a transcript of the proceedings of a symposium in which representatives of all the groups active in the early years gave accounts of their activities, entitled "A Difficult Dangerous Honesty", was published in 1987.

political status during 1978-81 was a time of crisis for feminism. During the no-wash protest of 1980, when the 30 women prisoners endured horrendous privations, there was massive international solidarity with their plight. It was a high point in terms of the numbers of groups in existence in the North, but there was a complete rift between the various viewpoints and the attempts that were made to engage in dialogue never succeeded in getting together all sections of the opposing viewpoints at the same time. Argument raged as to whether Armagh was a feminist issue, as some found themselves torn between support for the prisoners as women in distress and rejection of their republican politics. Hostilities were such that in the end there was little personal contact between groups. Since then the position has altered considerably. There are fewer all-purpose women's groups but many more community-based groups located within both nationalist and unionist areas. There are many single-issue groups campaigning for change — against rape, incest, battering, strip-searching of prisoners, for abortion rights, education facilities, improved health care — an endless list of demands relating to women's needs. There are also occasional contacts across the sectarian divide. These may be patchy, based on much compromise and words unspoken, with the fundamental contradictions always threatening to break through. Nevertheless they exist and one day it may be possible to develop a more radical and united movement.

In the 1970s few political organizations had begun to consider either the needs of their women members or the necessity of developing a political programme which would be relevant to women. Members of the Socialist Women's Group had held meetings with various organizations in an attempt to force the issue of women onto the agenda and they were appalled at the lack of interest they discovered. Peoples Democracy promised to develop a programme on women in three years time, once they had formulated a policy on the Soviet Union and other more pressing political issues. The republican movement had no progressive views on women other than on their ability to take part in the war effort and as late as 1974 had printed an article condemning "artificial" contraception and refused to publish a reply by a women's liberation group. Times have certainly changed. Women's sections in some form are now an integral part of political organizations and abortion is the only seriously contentious issue where women still have to win the final fight for the right to control their own bodies. None of this could have been achieved were it not for the persistent and unrelenting campaigning of feminists both within and without the various political organizations.

Despite all our achievements, however, the formation of an autonomous women's movement which would have the ability to unite women from all sections of the community and from all parts of the country remains as remote a prospect as ever. Efforts to establish feminist federations or to build all-Ireland support on issues such as the abortion referendum have met with only partial success. The stumbling block continues to be the crippling effect of Partition in leaving women from both sides of the Border suspicious of each other: the 26 counties fearful that they might get involved in controversy surrounding the war with Britain, the Unionist community in the 6 counties unwilling to offer solidarity with their sisters in the South because they are seen as part of a "foreign" country that is intent on annexing them against their will. And, it must also be said, Northern feminists have been suspicious of some of the attempts to set up 32 county structures because they have often been thinly disguised structures whose primary aim has been to bolster support for the national struggle. Until women can define their own priorities without reference to outside forces, true unity will never be possible. But this will not come about until a genuine process of discussion begins: one which will be honest about political differences and which will have as its fundamental core the desire to put forward the interests of all women, whether as prisoners, mothers, lesbians, workers, or any of the other roles undertaken by Irish women.

As the economy totters on the brink of bankruptcy and living conditions deteriorate, a war that no one can win continues. And women, who struggle to give life and to rear their children, continue to suffer and to mourn. As feminists we are not arguing for the passive demand of "peace" that the Peace Women, together with the churches, called for. We want something much more than that: an end to the patriarchal domination of women and an end to the capitalist system which sustains that patriarchy. In Ireland, that must also mean an end to British imperialist rule. A commitment to the priority of women's needs would be an important first step in asserting our independence from male-defined concerns and one that could ultimately lead to the creation of a movement which would have the potential to unite women from all over the country in a fight for a true liberation.

THE MEDIA:
ASKING THE RIGHT
QUESTIONS?

Ed Moloney was a student at Queen's University, Belfast, between 1966 and 1971 during the height of the civil rights campaign. In 1978 he joined *Hibernia* magazine as an assistant editor, and then worked for *The Irish Times*. Between 1981 and 1985 he was the paper's Northern editor and is currently Northern correspondent of the *Sunday Tribune*. He is co-author of *Paisley*, an unauthorised biography of the loyalist leader which was published in 1986.

It was a cold, boring Belfast Sunday afternoon in November 1968 (and how those Sundays could be boring) when the doorbell rang. I was one of a dozen or so, mostly English students living in what was known in those days as a Queen's University house — a terraced building converted into inexpensive but comfortable bed-sits — in Mount Charles in the heart of the university district.

Mount Charles is now one of Belfast's more select streets; in fact it's really a cul-de-sac and an exclusive one at that, a feature emphasised by the fancy gate at one end closing it off to traffic. Queen's, which once owned virtually the entire street, has encountered harsher days. The cruel effects of Mrs Thatcher's cuts have forced it to sell off property, mostly to the city's new yuppie class or to businesses. Property values have soared.

It's hard to believe now, but Mount Charles, with its tree-linked sidewalks and private park, was then a hive of student rebellion. Four or five doors away lived Kevin Boyle, then a young Law lecturer and one of the leaders of the newly-emerged Peoples Democracy, the mass, almost inchoate, student movement formed in the emotional wake of the 5 October civil rights demonstration in Derry. Meetings of the Peoples Democracy committee — the original "faceless" committee of ten elected to prevent the organization being swayed by the Young Socialists or other political activists — were held in his house and it was there that the plans were laid for some of the earliest civil rights agitation. There was much toing and froing between our house and his, not least because we owned the only accessible, working television set in the area and even in those early days everyone was addicted to news programmes.

It was Kevin at the door. Volunteers were needed to mount a picket outside the home of Bill Craig, the Stormont Minister of Home Affairs, he announced. Would we go? It was a welcome break from the tedium of a Belfast Sabbath, but we would have gone anyway. Bill Craig, more than any other Stormont politician, personified what we all saw as the bigotry and badness of the Unionist government. He had banned the 5 October march — seemingly in collusion with the Loyalist Apprentice Boys of Derry organization, which had threatened a counter-protest — and the blame for the RUC violence that followed was laid firmly at his door.

Some of us could remember an earlier demonstration outside Bill Craig's home in the autumn of 1967, when students had marched there to protest at the ban he had just slapped on the

Republican Clubs. The Republican Clubs were the new guise of Sinn Féin, then labouring under a proscription order. At the time nobody that I knew took seriously their claimed links with the IRA, or, if they did, cared that much about them. In those days, and for a long time during the civil rights agitation, most of us treated the IRA as something of a joke — a bunch of old men in trench-coats living off impossible dreams of what might have been. They weren't all like that, of course, and nor were they irrelevant. I certainly did not then know anything about the political re-thinking within the republican movement caused by the failure of the IRA's 1956-62 campaign and the resulting new political direction republicans had taken. We did not know that this new direction included republicans getting involved in civil rights agitation as the first stage of a process that would lead to Irish unity. Neither did we know any republicans personally — the odd veteran like Frank McGlade was pointed out at civil rights marches as a curiosity — and we did not even know of younger radicals like Joe McCann and Gerry Adams. It was one of the reasons we treated claims of an IRA hand behind the civil rights movement with such contempt. How could these old dodderers possibly be the scheming brains behind a movement that was so large and so broadly-based that it encompassed liberals, anarchists, socialists, confused radicals and conservative Catholics?

We were wrong, of course. Republicans were involved, and very deeply, as the subsequent telling of history has revealed. Many of the civil rights leaders knew all of this, but the bulk of student marchers did not know, chose not to see it, or if they did, did not care. Not that it would have mattered all that much had we been aware of the extent of republican involvement. Bill Craig and other Unionists might have been right in alleging an IRA hand in "the conspiracy", but "the conspiracy" would have got nowhere had the conditions which brought thousands of nationalists onto the streets not existed in the first place. And it was the existence of those conditions — discrimination, bad housing, gerrymandering etc. — which Unionists refused to concede.

We prided ourselves on our lack of bigotry. Anyone and everyone was welcome in our movement, provided they agreed with the civil rights demands. But we were aloof and elitist; the majority of us were privileged, middle class-aspiring students with little or no link with the people who had no votes, few jobs and who lived in the deplorable housing we chanted slogans about. The gulf between protesting students and the Protestant working class at that time is well known and documented — even though some of us did try to bridge it. We failed miserably, of course, but learned a useful lesson, one that has proved invaluable since, about the mind-boggling inflexibility of grass-roots loyalism. Less well known was the fact that an equally large gulf existed between most of us students and the Catholic working class whose conditions we were ostensibly trying to better. Like many of my contemporaries, I did not make my first visit to West Belfast until September 1969, and then only out of curiosity to see at first hand what a barricade looked like. Up to then I would have had problems finding the place. And so in those early months of 1968-69 many of us, more than would readily admit it nowadays, were campaigning in a vacuum.

The anti-Craig demonstration of 1967 had been a huge success. Thousands of us, Catholic and Protestant students together, had trooped up to his home carrying a coffin to symbolise the death of democracy. There had been talk of going to the Unionist Party headquarters in Glengall Street but these plans had been abandoned when a young, hotblooded, evangelical Protestant minister called Ian Paisley threatened a counter protest. I suppose we regarded Paisley with some of the same derision as we did the IRA; we nearly all dismissed him as a prehistoric throwback whose unrepresentative antics were, we assumed, being used by Stormont as an excuse to block us. Again we were wrong, as we were about the republicans, and badly misjudged the depth of his support, the paranoid nature of Unionism, and Paisley's unerring skill at exploiting it. But we were not alone in our misjudgement. So we had gone to Bill Craig's home instead, milled around outside waiting for something to happen, and when it did not we had all trooped back again to Queen's. A week later, in what now seems a remarkable coincidence, we had all gone out and voted in as president of the Students' Union the major organizer of the protest, an articulate and desperately radical figure called Rory — later "Red Rory" — McShane, now an eminently respectable — and not at all radical — solicitor in Newry, County Down.

That march had been my first ever political experience and had left two legacies both for me and for many of my Queen's contemporaries. It sent hot blood coursing through our veins and with it an unquenchable passion for politics; and it made

Bill Craig a natural target for student protest. Come 5 October 1968, and a student sit-down protest in Belfast's Linenhall Street a few days later, and the righteous anger flared in our breasts and we were all raring to go.

And so it was that ten minutes after Kevin Boyle's call to arms on that November Sunday, half a dozen of us were parading outside Bill Craig's large, affluent home carrying placards which captured the naïve innocence of our time. Some of the posters, designed by a printer who is now so respectable a figure in Belfast's business life that I won't embarrass him by naming him, featured a rough painted replica of that most Protestant of symbols, the Red Hand of Ulster, with the appropriate "one man, one vote" slogan underneath. Perhaps we, or the poster's designer, were trying to be ironic, but I don't think so. It was one of many indications that for the bulk of the student civil rights activists, what was going on was about justice and democracy *within* Northern Ireland, *within* the constitutional status quo, and had little to do with nationalism or republicanism. If anything, we were trying to make Northern Ireland more British, not less.

Not everyone saw it that way, of course. For some, like the republicans, the civil rights campaign was only part of a much larger battle. The first time I can remember realising that was at the Armagh march in November 1968, when a row broke out over a Peoples Democracy' leaflet which referred to injustices in the city of "Londonderry" (in those early days the notion that one could woo, or at least not alienate Protestants by adopting Unionist language and symbols was strong). But those elements with a more far-reaching agenda were regarded as unrepresentative and small — which, I still believe, they were. The bulk of the civil rights supporters adopted an attitude which today could happily, if somewhat ironically, grace the platform of a Unionist supporter of integration with Britain, like Bob McCartney, head of the Campaign for Equal Citizenship: "If Northern Ireland insists on being British, then it must accept British standards". This non-nationalist, non-republican character of the civil rights movement was something which Unionists, to their cost, were never able or willing to understand.

Nor did they understand — then or since — the scorn with which the Southern state was viewed by many of the student protesters. One perhaps apocryphal story that did the rounds in my circle summed it all up. It concerned Bernadette Devlin and her then boyfriend, a character from Dublin, I believe, who rejoiced in the name of Michael Collins. They had both been on the 5 October protest in Derry and after the police had run amok they had both fled to Donegal where, as soon as they crossed the border, Michael Collins had said something like: "Isn't it great to breathe the air of freedom again?" The story, as we heard and repeated it approvingly, was that Bernadette gave him an earful about some of the political and historical realities of Southern society: its gombeen, pork-barrel politics, its corruption, its dominance by a quasi-medieval Catholic church, and so on. It really was the case with many of us that as soon as we had sorted out the North, the South would be next.

Naïvety was the name of the game for the foot-soldiers of the civil rights campaign, those with no natural talent for or interest in the conspiratorial intricacies of politics. And so that Sunday afternoon, none of us wondered why we had been summoned out to Bill Craig's house; we just went. Within half an hour the scales were lifted when there appeared down the street a BBC television and radio crew, summoned by a phone call from Mount Charles before our departure. A young Martin Bell (now a senior British television reporter) interviewed us on the street and we made both radio and TV news programmes that night.

It was my first, but by no means my last lesson in media manipulation. Sunday is a bad day for news, so if you can stage something like a picket or demonstration and link it in with possible forthcoming events — like the civil rights marches which were then taking place every two or three weeks — you'll be made. If you don't get coverage that day, copy-starved newspapers will gobble you up for Monday. (The reverse is also true, as the authorities and others in the North have learned. If you have some distasteful or embarrassing news to announce, make sure you do it late on Friday evening or Saturday afternoon. It will be too late for most of the next day's papers, too complicated for the weekend TV and radio news slots, and too out of date for Monday morning. One way or another, the coverage is likely to be minimal.)

The civil rights leaders were good at handling the media. They understood how radio, television and the print media worked and what their needs were in a way which Unionists, even to this day, have never really mastered. But that neat little PR trick outside Bill Craig's house, like dozens of others, worked well largely because whoever set it up knew he or she could rely on a sympathetic response from the BBC. The civil rights movement had by that stage won the media war in Britain — which at that time was where it mattered. The bulk of the media saw the Unionists as bigoted and antediluvian in much the same way as the South African regime is viewed now (Rupert Murdoch's papers notwithstanding). Their leaders were at best "ineffectual or cowardly" like the reforming Terence O'Neill, "duplicitous" like Brian Faulkner, "bullying and oafish" like Ian Paisley, or "sinister" like Bill Craig. The civil rights campaigners were in contrast bathed by the media in a white light of righteousness. They were articulate, fair, honest, decent, generous and with right on their side — all the things the Unionists were not: the goodies versus the Prod baddies. Some of the civil rights leaders, like John Hume and Gerry Fitt, made such a remarkably favourable impression on the media that it has stood them in good stead for the rest of their political lives.

There were good reasons for all of this. Northern nationalists had given up expecting change to come via Dublin's efforts (something that has left a resentment in the Northern psyche so deep that Southern politicians would be ill-advised to ignore it) and had turned instead to Britain as the agent of change. The British Labour Party and the trade union movement were cultivated by nationalists like Gerry Fitt, and the tactic paid dividends; their efforts created a reservoir of support in the ranks of the Labour movement at just the right moment. Times were changing in Britain: 13 years of Tory rule came to an end during the early '60s, progressive politics came to the fore, and increased affluence also made for an exploitable conscience. But perhaps prime amongst all these factors was the shock caused among British people, particularly the liberal establishment, by the discovery in the mid to late '60s that a political sewer existed in their backyard. The shock deepened when they began to realise that not only had Britain tolerated the situation in Northern Ireland for years, but at times had actually gone out of its way to do nothing about it.

Awareness of the Northern state dawned slowly, first with incomprehension at an outbreak of rioting in Belfast's Divis Street in 1964 and then with worry and concern at the Unionist government's over-reaction to the 1966 Easter Rising commemorations and at the Malvern Street killings by the revived Ulster Volunteer Force, also in 1966. Interest in the North slowly fermented — good journalists sniffed a damned good story and, what's more, one that was right on their doorsteps. Their interest was to culminate in the mould-breaking journalism of people like Mary Holland in the *Observer* and the then pre-Murdoch *Sunday Times*. They helped set the agenda and the atmosphere for other newspapers, the BBC and the Independent Television networks at a time when investigative, campaigning journalism and TV current affairs programmes were coming into vogue. And it was not simply a case of journalists automatically sympathising with the underdog — in this case the Catholics. Some of the best stories, like the *Sunday Times* "John Bull's Other Island", were meticulously and objectively researched and well written, displaying all that's best in the craft of journalism.

So, when the civil rights movement started to articulate its unanswerable case both on the streets and — as crucially — on the television, the Unionists had lost the game, as they deserved to. A substantial body of political opinion in Britain already supported the aims of the civil rights movement and the Unionists' only potential allies in Britain, those in the Tory party, for example, either disowned them or were too embarrassed to speak up for them. It only needed an inquiring, probing media to finish the job. Within weeks of 5 October, the Northern Ireland of one-party Stormont rule had been tried and found guilty. It is impossible to exaggerate the influence of the media on all of this. It helped expose Northern Ireland's political wrongs to the world, gave civil rights leaders an invaluable platform (which they were more than capable of using) and added enormously to the political pressure in Britain for action. Without that media attention, it is doubtful whether the campaign would have been half as successful.

It has now become a cliché to ask whether those of us who sat chanting slogans in Linenhall Street in October 1968 had any inkling that we were on the brink of two decades of violence. Of course we did not, and in retrospect we had every reason not to think that we were. None of us expected, or believed, that the problem would be allowed to fester for so long. It is comforting now, for some, to say that we all underestimated the intractability of the problem, understated the capacity for violence and were naïve in expecting a peaceful, speedy "solution" to what is, after all, an "insoluble problem". But after 20 years of instability, of social and political dislocation and innumerable deaths and injuries are we not also entitled to ask why it has been allowed to last so long? If the violence we in the North have experienced had happened, say, in Britain, would it have been allowed to go on? Would not the equivalent toll in Britain (over 85,000 deaths), or in the USA (nearly 500,000 deaths), have been seen for what it was: a major political cataclysm requiring in-depth analysis and drastic remedy? If that is true for those countries, why not for Northern Ireland? And if so, should we not therefore also question many of the assumptions about Northern Ireland, assumptions that have led so many for so long to accept that what exists here is an "insoluble problem" with roots too deep and obscure for rational examination?

Here, as elsewhere, journalists have a bounden duty to question assumptions, to keep asking why, to explain. We are, or we should be, in a combative, questioning relationship with every person and agency we deal with. That is a guiding rule that should apply to political parties and to paramilitary groups equally. But, above all, it should apply to government and to official information outlets upon which most journalists, and the reading and viewing public they service, rely. Too often it does not and for that we may have paid a dear price.

There is no room here for an exhaustive analysis of the media's performance in Northern Ireland, even if such a thing were feasible. Nor is it possible to give blanket judgements, since there have been, and continue to be, exceptions to the rule. But it is possible, nevertheless, to discern two major phases in the British, Irish and international media's coverage of the North. The first lasted from 1968 until 1974 and was characterised by all the healthier aspects of journalism — curiosity, indignation, scepticism, and a wish to inform and explain. True, there was a lot going on then and most of it was new, exciting and challenging: the arrival of British troops, street violence, the birth of the Provisional IRA, internment, the IRA's bombing campaign, Bloody Sunday, the genesis of loyalist revolt and paramilitaries like the UDA, Direct Rule and so on. There was plenty for young, ambitious journalists to get stuck into. Northern Ireland was *the* place for a reporter to cut his or her teeth, as a casual glance at, for instance, the subsequent careers of Fleet Street's then team in Belfast will confirm. True there was also a lot of bad journalism in that period; unthinking jingoistic rubbish, the re-hashed ramblings of official and unofficial PR men, but, to give only one example, it was the heyday of the *Sunday Times* reportage of Northern Ireland, characterised best of all by the Insight team's objective, informative account of the birth of the IRA and the genesis of the Troubles. It was a time, then, when many journalists felt it obligatory to question all assumptions, particularly those handed down by the people in power.

The turning point probably came with the success of the Ulster Workers' Council strike and the collapse of the power-sharing Sunningdale experiment. In many ways Sunningdale was the climax of the previous six years and its failure seemed to confirm the hopelessness of the problem, underlining what appeared to be an essential truth — that there was no solution. It also came after six long years of violent conflict — as long as the Second World War — and people in the South of Ireland and Britain were getting bored by it all. In the South they were also getting worried. The Troubles in the North were too close to home for comfort.

If anything characterises British media coverage from then on, it is probably the weary belief that Northern Ireland was essentially an intractable community relations problem. It consisted of two sets of mutually incompatible Paddies, who were both wedded hopelessly to "mindless" violence and separated only by the British government, an essentially neutral and benevolent arbitrator. In the South the atmosphere was a good deal nastier. Conor Cruise O'Brien began collecting files on "subversive elements" in the media, Section 31 of the Broadcasting Act came into its own and revisionism gained ground rapidly. Devoid of a liberal tradition and with a history of using force to quell dissent, the South lapsed into intolerance, encouraging the view that the symptom of the problem — republican violence — was its cause. As the Troubles dragged on through the '70s and into the next decade, the assumption that Northern Ireland was "an insoluble problem" dominated the media. There were exceptions to the rule, most ·of them in British commercial television, but their influence was limited, while in the South, the mentality spawned by Section 31 encouraged at an alarming pace the view that to cover anything outside of constitutional politics was tantamount to declaring sympathy for subversive groups. At a time when the media's standards were anyhow beginning to drop alarmingly, in Britain it became commonplace for the popular, and increasingly the serious print media to invent stories about Northern Ireland.

Abroad the almost universal view was that Northern Ireland was not a political problem — not a problem about power and who controls or does not control it — but a community relations problem, whose solution lay in the realm of religious ecumenism and integrated education. Until the 1981 hunger strikes, Britain was viewed as a neutral party trying helplessly to get the warring Paddies to live together like normal human beings. American journalists visiting Northern Ireland on fact-finding missions regularly asked the Northern Ireland Office to arrange their itineraries — a degree of collusion with government they would automatically baulk at in any other of the world's trouble spots.

For reasons that are understandable, and for others that are inexcusable, analysis and explanation gave way to plain untrammelled reporting. Northern Ireland became a simple violence story as predictable, regular and despairingly intractable as the Middle East. In Britain people were bored with Northern Ireland — it was an issue on which there was a large measure of consensus at Westminster, and it was successfully removed from the domestic political agenda by "Ulsterisation", i.e. the gradual replacement of British soldiers by local, mostly Protestant forces, who from then on bore the bulk of the casualties. In the South there was no less a lack of interest — Northern Ireland rarely impinged on political consciousness unless it threatened (as it did during the 1981 prison protests) to spill over the Border. All the while the violence continued, albeit at a much lower level than in the early '70s, and all the while political settlement looked as elusive as ever. But few bothered to ask or explain why; or to wonder how long it could continue like that before something, somewhere blew a gasket; or to question the government's role.

In some ways it is understandable that the media took to reporting rather than analysing and explaining. To begin with it was easier, particularly when there was no shortage of government and non-government agencies pumping out material, to re-write the news from these sources. It was also safer. To attempt to explain why the violence continued so relentlessly meant subjecting paramilitary groups to minute examination: What support did they have? What sort of people joined their ranks and why? What were their goals, their methods? Was what the government, army and police said about them true? And if not, what was the truth? With some notable exceptions — a few journalists who attempted to keep the North's problems on the agenda — there was little interest in Britain in asking those questions, never mind answering them. The predominant view was that "Ulster" was insoluble, the government was doing its best and the major obstacle to progress was the IRA, an essentially unrepresentative conspiracy led by greedy, racketeering "godfathers" who forced their will on a cowed, frightened host population. In the South, to ask those questions carried another risk — that of being labelled a sympathiser. For in some powerful minds, to write knowledgeably about groups like the IRA (and it has also happened, albeit to a lesser degree, to journalists writing about loyalist groups) implied a degree of intimacy with them virtually inseparable from outright support. Careful, ambitious journalists learned either to ditch their objectivity and approach subjects like the IRA with outright hostility, or to avoid the subject altogether.

The gasket finally blew in 1981 and 1982, first with the prison hunger strikes and then with Sinn Féin's intervention at the ballot box. The latter's success took nearly all the media by surprise and most sought refuge in the emotional upheaval that accompanied the procession of prison deaths to explain it. There was obviously some truth in that, but it was surely insufficient. After all, the IRA had re-grouped and re-organized after the setbacks of the Roy Mason era (the hardline Labour Northern Secretary in the late '70s) long before the hunger strikes. Equally it had also been able to sustain an illegal armed conspiracy, constantly replenishing its ranks with new young recruits, for years beforehand, despite all the power and strength that the British state could muster. Why had the IRA managed to survive for 13 years, as it was then; nearly 20 years now? What persuades young people to join its ranks in such numbers, risking imprisonment, even death? What makes countless others give its members refuge, supply hiding places for its guns and bombs or give vital information to its leaders?

Journalists automatically ask similar questions in other areas of strife, from the inner city areas of Dublin and England to Central America and the Middle East. In Northern Ireland was it really a case of the "godfathers" browbeating their people, or were there political factors at work, objective reasons explaining why otherwise normal, family-loving people could feel so antagonistic to the state and its agencies that they were prepared to countenance and support killing? The answer is obvious and with it the explanation for the length of the North's agony. It would be trite to single out any single culprit to blame for why it has lasted so long, but inevitably one wonders whether, if the media had been as industriously probing and sceptical as it should have been — as it was during the early days of the Troubles — our strife would have lasted quite as long.

Those events in the early '80s began a third phase of the media's coverage of Northern Ireland, one which resembled the healthy days of the '60s and early '70s. Old assumptions were questioned because they had to be; because the basis for them manifestly no longer existed. How, for instance, could people claim that "the men of violence" forced themselves on their own people when, in the privacy and secrecy of the ballot box, those people cast their votes for them? How could the British government be cast as the benevolently neutral referee when the links between political attitudes and the government's security, social and economic policies were so obvious? And if those links did exist, how was it possible to sustain any longer the idea that a bit more religious or educational ecumenism could solve the problem? The questions were there begging to be asked and answered and, by and large, the media lived up to its duty. And with that sort of coverage came, by no coincidence, a new spurt of political realism.

For the first time in over a decade journalists and politicians were forced to question why so many people supported organizations like the IRA. What was there about British policies in the security and economic fields, in the behaviour of the British army, the RUC, the UDR, the courts and the Unionists that led thousands of normal and otherwise peaceable people to believe that the only way to deal with them was through the bomb and the bullet? Was this a new phenomenon brought about by Britain's handling of the hunger strikes or something that had been there all the time — hidden, camouflaged, festering, and wished away or deliberately ignored?

To pose questions like those and to seek answers is the journalist's job. And likewise with the "solutions" — such as the Anglo-Irish Agreement — that politicians propose. But there are disquieting signs that this phase could be short-lived, that too many in the media have uncritically accepted the Agreement as the panacea that politicians have claimed it to be, or have succumbed to the unspoken charge that to question its performance is tantamount to subversion. Either way reality is once more threatened by distortion. Much blood was shed and many lives lost before the media regained its proper inquisitiveness. Is it always going to be like that? In ten or 20 years time will there be another book like this, commemorating, or mourning, our endless journey?

LAW AND DISORDER

Eilis McDermott was born in Derry in 1950 and educated at Rathmore Grammar School, Belfast, and Queen's University, Belfast. She joined Peoples Democracy while at Queen's and in 1969 went to America as part of a NICRA delegation to collect funds for rebuilding houses destroyed in the August 1969 pogroms on Catholic areas. She has been a lawyer since 1974 and was involved in some of the major "supergrass" trials of the early '80s. She is married and lives in Belfast with her three children.

I was helping Billy Butlin to expand his empire when the first civil rights march took place from Coalisland to Dungannon in August 1968. I was not in Duke Street in Derry on 5 October either but a few days later, in my first week at Queen's University, Belfast, I did not take much coaxing to become a student protester. It was the thing to do in 1968 and I had all the props — black polo neck jumper and white face make-up — for the role. Fred Taggart, president of the Queen's students' union was our Danny the Red (Daniel Cohn Bendit, one of the most publicised leaders of the Paris student uprising in May 1968). We students were filled with outrage at the RUC attack on the 5 October march, but there was also a feeling of hope and energy, a feeling that, whatever was wrong, we were going to sort it out. Speaking for myself and, I suspect, the majority of the several thousand students on our march towards Belfast City Hall, the fact that we had no real knowledge of the politics of Northern Ireland did not detract from our enthusiasm.

I was born in Derry City in 1950, the eldest of six children. We moved to Liverpool a few years later and then to Belfast in 1961. My father decided we should live in what is now West Belfast (it was never called that then) to avoid the possibility of loyalist attacks. He told us about the murder of the MacMahon family who were killed by a murder gang, generally believed to be police in disguise, in one of the most notorious episodes of the "Troubles" when the state was set up in 1922. I thought he was living in the past and being unnecessarily alarmist. My seven years at a convent school on the outskirts of Belfast did nothing to change that view; it was an upbringing as sheltered from the sectarian realities of Northern Ireland as it was possible to get. We children were encouraged to do our best at school and the educational opportunities open to us, opportunities which previous generations did not have, were emphasised. My schoolfriends and I did not in any way consider ourselves to be second-class citizens — youthful confidence was not in short supply. We mixed, especially in our senior years, with boys and girls from other Catholic schools and from state (i.e. Protestant) schools. The only division we perceived as relevant in 1968 was the one between young and old.

This was all very well and no doubt a credit to my teachers but it was poor preparation for being prevented by hundreds of policemen from marching to the City Hall in one's own city on that Wednesday afternoon in October 1968. I was genuinely mystified when we were not allowed to go any further than Linenhall Street. We sat on the ground within sight of the City Hall. There was no question of violence — the demonstration was quite good-humoured. There was no counter-demonstration, just a handful of loyalists waving flags. As it became clear that it was not a mistake and that the serried ranks of riot-helmeted police were going to stay there as long as we did, puzzlement gave way to indignation and determination. The determination, as we trudged back to Queen's in the rain, was not that the Border between the North and South of Ireland should go, or that every man should have a vote, but that we *would* get to the City Hall.

Peoples Democracy was formed that night. There was standing room only in the MacMordie Hall of the Queen's students' union (now the Mandela Hall). I remember Ciaran McKeown, later one of the leaders of the Peace People organization, calling for a moratorium on protests which, judging by the laughter it provoked, did not accord with the mood of the audience. It was agreed that anyone could be a member of Peoples Democracy so long as they thought everyone should have a vote, a job and a house, that the Special Powers Act should be repealed and the B Specials should be disbanded. In theory five people could make a decision in the name of the Peoples Democracy just as well as five hundred. There were no membership cards or subscription fees. Everyone was welcome — the more the merrier.

The six demands adopted by Peoples Democracy: one man, one vote; fair (electoral) boundaries; houses on need; jobs on merit; free speech; repeal of the Special Powers Act, seemed exceedingly modest. They would surely present no problem to a government willing to listen to its citizens and change with the times. No one in that hall would have believed that 20 years on the problems at the root of those demands would remain just as resistant as ever to a solution within the structure of the state. That lives would be lost in the events that would follow was unthinkable. I am sure we were, to a man and woman, anti-war and from the start it was taken for granted that marches and demonstrations would be non-violent. This applied, of course, not just to Peoples Democracy, who were mostly students, but to the more broadly-based Northern Ireland Civil Rights Association (NICRA). Martin Luther King was the inspiration of the movement and the songs of the US civil rights movement were much in use. Occasionally there were academic arguments within

Peoples Democracy about what one was entitled to do to defend oneself but no one sought to derogate from the principle of non-violence.

For an organization without rules and so dependent on spontaneity, Peoples Democracy worked quite hard. A "Faceless Committee" was elected to do what organizing there was to be done, and it debated matters of state far into the night. Since I was too faceless even to be on the faceless committee I drew slogans on placards. Every Saturday a caravan of beaten-up cars set off for a provincial town to spread the Peoples Democracy message. We were received enthusiastically — especially, at times, by our opponents. Of course, the local people in these towns, especially the older ones, needed no instruction from the likes of me about the reality of life in Northern Ireland, but many of them seemed genuinely pleased and hopeful because their grievances were being taken up by a new generation and, more importantly, in a new way. The message not to be afraid; that we would win with words because fairness and justice were on our side, had a forceful attraction. In Omagh, County Tyrone, we were told by the RUC that we were going to be run out of town by men with cudgels. And when we were, it did not occur to any of us to suggest that they should be prosecuted.

The ideal of civil rights had taken root. On 16 November 1968 I thought Craigavon Bridge in Derry would creak under the weight of women with prams and small children, people in wheelchairs, teenagers, thin men with no jobs, big mountainy men in their good suits, students, teachers, 15,000 strong, singing "We Shall Overcome", as a second civil rights march was held along the route of the 5 October one. I was not in the flippant mood of five weeks before. Here were those who knew about gerrymandering, sectarian policies in housing and employment, and repressive legislation. A Unionist politician of the time used to say of the civil rights movement: "They have unleashed a monster they cannot control". I do not remember anyone ever asking him who had created the monster.

There was wide news coverage of the civil rights marches and our passive resistance to the RUC when we were not allowed into the centre of various towns. It still seemed to me that the movement's demands were so basic that all the trouble would be over by Christmas and I confidently predicted as much when I spoke to students' unions in England which had now become interested in our civil rights campaign. It seemed reasonable to hope that however intransigent the Unionist government was, they might be persuaded to embark on a programme of reform at least for the sake of their reputation internationally. But, of course, it was not all over by Christmas.

The Peoples Democracy march from Belfast to Derry that set out on New Year's Day 1969 went ahead in spite of the moratorium on marches agreed to in the wake of Prime Minister Terence O'Neill's plea for calm. But marching through Mid-Ulster and South Derry — territory unknown to me — I was struck by the support and encouragement we received; the march grew bigger every day and local people offered food and shelter to marchers who were total strangers to them. Peoples Democracy's differences with NICRA were forgotten too when we were attacked at Burntollet, apparently with the collusion of the RUC. Again it seems strange, in retrospect, that no one called for our attackers to be prosecuted although the entire episode was recorded on film. Being hit by a brick during the ambush at Burntollet bridge seems pretty small beer nowadays, but it showed me for the first time the depth of hatred and fear that existed amongst a section of the Unionist population. Our arrival in Derry on 4 January was emotional and when we heard the next day that houses in the Bogside had been wrecked during the night by RUC men I was somehow not surprised. It was slowly dawning on me that by demanding elementary reform we were — without meaning to be — a threat to the state.

It was common at the time to hear Queen's University described by members of the Unionist government as a "hotbed of republicanism". I did not know anyone at that time who was a republican. My view was that whatever the merits of the Anglo-Irish Treaty in 1921, I was now a British citizen; indeed I had applied for a British passport in 1967 and the Border was of no more than academic interest to me. We were constantly and sincerely, though rather pathetically it now seems, asking to be treated the same as people in Yorkshire. Even on the march to Derry one of our number who produced an Irish tricolour when we were crossing the bridge over the river Bann at Toomebridge not only had it summarily removed, but was laughed at by the marchers.

Burntollet undoubtedly increased support and several Peoples Democracy candidates did well in elections to the Stormont parliament in February 1969. Bernadette Devlin's victory when she won the Mid-Ulster seat in the Westminster parliament that

April was momentous. Her ability and charisma, the great media interest, her spell-binding maiden speech — surely now there would have to be movement by the Stormont government. On top of that NICRA, Peoples Democracy, the Nationalist Party MPs, Gerry Fitt and Paddy Kennedy of the Republican Labour Party and Paddy Devlin and Vivian Simpson of the Northern Ireland Labour Party were all backing the civil rights demands.

But the rage which had been burning in loyalist areas erupted in August 1969. Tension had been building up for days. I was in Albert Street in the Lower Falls area of Belfast, by myself, when the shooting started. A woman pulled me in her door and, despite a pathological fear of dogs, I lay on the floor clutching her labrador. She had recognised me from seeing me on television. She would not let me go until she thought it was safe and as she let me out, she said: "Look what you've started, daughter". I ran back to Queen's feeling bitterly angry and ashamed. I knew we had not "started" anything and I knew she had not meant it that way, but there was something very shaming about having been involved in some way in defenceless people being shot dead. No one was shooting in University Road.

I was relieved when the British army came in, although, as the wise predicted, no good was to come of it. In November 1969 I went to America as part of a NICRA delegation to collect money for rebuilding the houses burnt out in the August pogroms. I incurred the wrath of one Irish county association by mentioning the slums on the Shankill Road as well as the Falls Road, our attitude being that the relationship of the Protestant working class to the Catholics was that of "three ha'pence looking down on a penny". Having regard to what we were collecting for and the close proximity of the events, this was looked on as an indiscretion on my part. The situation was only retrieved by the exercise of the considerable diplomatic talents of the late Frank Gogarty, then chairman of NICRA. We were there mainly to attend a big conference in New York, but I stayed on to go to other meetings. I was invited to meet the Black Panthers in Boston. The Black Panther Party was a flamboyantly militant offshoot from the Student Non-Violent Coordinating Committee which had been active in the US civil rights movement. When I arrived for our meeting I was ushered into a back room hung with bandoliers and posters urging "Seize the Time" and "Free Huey Newton" (one of the Panther leaders). I was kept waiting for a time appropriate to my station but eventually three leather-clad

Panthers appeared from behind the backdrop and sat, arms folded, on a table in front of me. A long silence was broken with: "Now you're here, sister, aren't you going to say anything?" After I had spoken briefly there were some informed questions and as I was leaving they told me they had made me an honorary Black Panther sister.

Those were the beginnings of my involvement in the civil rights campaign as far as I was concerned. Now no one living in Northern Ireland can look back over the last 20 years without an almost unbearable sadness and I am no different. We look back from different standpoints and my particular interest has been the law and how the executive has used and abused it to fit the requirements of the political situation.

It is beyond dispute that the state of Northern Ireland was born in violence and the threat of violence. Nor is it a matter of argument that a substantial minority of the citizens of the state have never accepted its validity, nor even accepted that they are citizens of it (something the law allows them to do). In every decade there has been violence directed against the state. Emergency legislation has been a constant feature of the North's legal system — we live in an emergency that has now lasted for almost 70 years. Clearly the reason for the emergency legislation is that the existence of the state does not have the consent of sufficient of the governed. This has been the case since the passing of the Government of Ireland Act in 1920 and is likely to remain so for as long as the basic political problem is unresolved.

The old Special Powers Act of the Stormont government at least acknowledged, by implication, that the reason for the witholding of the minority's consent to be governed by the state was political and that the violence that was periodically directed against the state was designed to bring about political change. It was passed in 1922 and gave the Minister of Home Affairs authority "to take all such steps ... as may be necessary for preserving peace and maintaining order". The Act conferred wide powers of arrest, questioning, search and detention on the police. It also allowed for internment which was used whenever the state appeared to be under threat. Internment was an executive rather than a judicial power; the authority to intern people, or release them from confinement, lay with the Minister of Home Affairs. The Act made no attempt to disguise what was going on under a facade of normality or to pretend that due legal process was being observed when it was not.

Even when reforms were brought in for the first time — after the civil rights campaign — aimed at ensuring that the minority population received equal treatment before the law, the Special Powers remained in force. Now, however, the period of internment without trial introduced in 1971 under the premiership of Brian Faulkner attracted considerable national and international opprobrium. The first few days of internment saw unprecedented violence as well as total confusion as to the whereabouts of the arrested persons. Many were to be officially "lost" for over a week. Eventually the Nissen huts at an old airfield at Long Kesh were filled up, there was a prison ship in Belfast harbour, women were interned in a wing of Armagh Prison. It soon became apparent that many of the people arrested in the internment swoops were not even suspected of paramilitary involvement — some were political activists, others were completely uninvolved. Seventeen-year-olds and younger were taken from their homes and "detained" — as it became officially known in 1972 — in one of many attempts to disguise the real nature of repressive measures by changing their names. In the first six months of internment 2,357 persons were arrested.

Against that background Bloody Sunday in Derry in January 1972, and the Widgery Report which whitewashed the role of the British troops who shot dead 13 civilians, dealt a mortal blow to any hope of a peaceful resolution of our problems. Stormont fell in March 1972, violence escalated and it must have been crystal clear to the British government that the policy of continued internment was politically and militarily self-defeating. Yet they continued it under successive Secretaries of State, interning a total of over 2,000 people until internment was finally phased out in December 1975.

In 1973, however, the Northern Ireland (Emergency Provisions) Act was passed, following a report by a committee under Lord Diplock. It replaced the Special Powers Act while keeping many of its powers, including the power to intern, or "detain", without trial. The new Act passed all the necessary stages in parliament very speedily. As a footnote in the margins of history it is interesting that at the committee stage of the Bill it was proposed that since jury trial was to be abolished for politically motivated offences, such cases should be tried by three judges. The committee split evenly on the proposal, which was defeated by the chairman's casting vote. (The introduction of three-judge courts was one of the changes in the system of justice which has been sought unsuccessfully by the Irish government through the Anglo-Irish Agreement.)

The Emergency Provisions Act was to dramatically change the mode of trial for certain specified offences. Juries were abolished, there was no longer a right to bail, the burden of proof in effect shifted to the accused in cases of possession of firearms or explosives, powers to stop, search and seize were extended and the law relating to the admissibility of confessions was drastically altered. It was in the last area that the changes were to be felt most keenly. Under common law the Crown had to satisfy the court that any alleged confession was made voluntarily. Under the new provisions a confession was assumed to be voluntary unless the accused could show that it had been obtained by torture, or inhuman or degrading treatment. What a severe level of ill-treatment an accused person had to establish is indicated by the fact that the European Court of Human Rights, in the case brought by the Irish government against Britain, found that the "hooded men" who had been subjected to food and sleep deprivation, white noise, long periods of standing with arms outstretched against walls, and kept with hoods over their heads for seven days, had not been tortured — although the court did find that they had been subjected to "inhuman and degrading treatment".

Under the new Act the British army was given the power to detain a suspect for up to four hours, and both army and police were empowered to stop and question any person as to his or her identity and knowledge of terrorist activity. On top of that the police could arrest anyone they suspected of being a terrorist and detain them for up to 72 hours, and they were not required to show any reasonable grounds for their suspicion. Between 1978 and 1980 the number of persons detained for more than four hours under the Emergency Provisions Act and the Prevention of Terrorism Act (brought in in the wake of the Birmingham bombings in 1974) more than doubled. Police powers of arrest under criminal law have been superseded by the power to arrest "on suspicion" under the emergency legislation, indicating the way in which emergency provisions become the norm.

A more sinister feature of their use also became apparent. Suspects could be held for up to seven days at holding centres at Castlereagh and Gough Barracks which specifically catered for intensive interrogations. There were frequent complaints and a widespread belief that suspects were being ill-treated as a matter of policy to get them to make statements. In turn the reputation gained by Castlereagh and Gough made it more likely that a suspect would be frightened into making a false confession even without physical ill-treatment. Where serious injuries were found it was suggested that they were self-inflicted in order to have the suspect's alleged statement ruled inadmissible in court. In one case a doctor who had examined two suspects said they would need to be "stoics" to inflict upon themselves the injuries they exhibited. He said he had never met a stoic in all his years of medical practice, yet he was being asked to accept that he had met two within the space of half an hour in Castlereagh.

Between 1976 and '79, 85% of convictions in the Diplock courts were based solely on confessions. The law did not admit of any distinction between signed confessions and alleged verbal admissions. Michael Culbert, who was accused of the murder of an RUC man in 1978, was questioned for very lengthy periods without a break, a fact that was not disputed. For much of the time he had been made to stand. He had not answered any questions for six days, but on the last day of his seven day detention period the Crown claimed he had made a fairly lengthy verbal admission to the murder. The detectives interviewing him did not write anything down until they had left the interview room because, they said, they did not want to interrupt the flow of his confession. They claimed that what they did write down then was a verbatim account of what he had said. The accused man never acknowledged the alleged confession in any way. Professor John Dugard, Professor of Law at the University of Witwatersrand, who was sent by Amnesty International to observe the appeal in that case, remarked that even in South Africa a verbal admission is not evidence against an accused unless he or she adopts it at the first appearance in court.

Raymond McCartney, accused of murder in 1977, alleged he had been ill-treated (and two of the men arrested with him were the two "stoics" referred to earlier.) In his case the caution which is read out to suspects had been initialled but the body of the statement he was alleged to have made was unacknowledged in any way. What would a dispassionate jury have made of those cases? It was parliament, not the judges, which made this law, but one of the safeguards of the jury system is that it is always open to a juror to refuse to convict if he or she considers the law to be unjust.

In 1979 Amnesty International produced a report saying that "maltreatment of suspected terrorists by the RUC has taken place with sufficient frequency to warrant ... a public inquiry".[1] The Amnesty report was supported by the evidence of two doctors, one in Belfast and one in Armagh, who had examined suspects on behalf of the police. As a result of this evidence the British government was forced to commission the Bennett Report, which concluded that "a number of prisoners had received injuries which were not self-inflicted and were sustained during the period of detention at a police office".[2] The Bennett Report made recommendations for the future but the system of ill-treatment to secure confessions had by force of circumstances come to an end.

Between 1981 and 1985 the police used the evidence of alleged accomplices to secure convictions in the Diplock courts or at least to keep accused persons in custody for a substantial period until the time of their trial. It is not now denied by the Northern Ireland Office that this was indeed the system although for some time it was maintained that the procession of supergrasses (as most people called them) willing to give evidence against alleged former colleagues in illegal organizations was a series of happy coincidences for the authorities. The police also for some considerable time publicly maintained the fiction that the supergrasses were "converted terrorists" who were now, at least by implication, opposed to violence and anxious to do what they could to stop it.

The reality was rather less uplifting. From the time that the supergrass went into police custody until the day he had to appear in court to give evidence a very lengthy period of time elapsed (one or two years in most cases). During that time he was either with police at a secret address or in a special wing of the prison receiving very frequent visits from senior police officers (with whom all supergrasses seemed to be on first-name terms). They had to rely on the police for everything and saw no one without the express approval of the police. Their own mothers could not visit them. One senior solicitor was moved to remark that if the defence were to adopt similar tactics in relation to a witness they

1. Amnesty International, *Report of an Amnesty International mission to Northern Ireland.* London, June 1978.
2. *Report of the Committee of Inquiry into Police Interrogation Procedures in Northern Ireland.* London: HMSO 1979, Cmd. 7497.

would be charged with conspiring to pervert the course of justice. All this, allied to the fact that they had received either immunity from prosecution or the promise of an early release (which was denied officially, but two have been released already) and the fact that after the trial was over they would still have to rely on the authorities to be resettled in another country with a new identity gave them an incentive to lie which made their evidence suspect from the start.

Although they invariably appeared in court well dressed and groomed, to such an extent that they were sometimes not initially recognised by former acquaintances, many had unsavoury backgrounds. Two had been paid agents of the Special Branch of the RUC before their "conversion". One of those had been discharged from the British army as an alleged psychopath and the other was described by the judge as being a man to whose lips a lie came more easily than the truth. In neither case was their evidence accepted, but the accused had already been in custody for more than two years.

It was virtually impossible, in most cases, to counter the charges. For the most part the supergrass would allege that an accused had attended meetings with him where murders or bombings were discussed but which, for some reason, were never implemented. It was possible for a charge to read "That you ... between January and May 1982 conspired with persons unknown to wound a person unknown". Even if one could tie down the date it was impossible to make the defence of alibi where the times were not and could not, with precision, be given (unless, as in one case, an accused was able to show that he was actually in prison when he was alleged to have been planning a particular crime).

There was rarely corroboration of the supergrass's evidence. In Scotland, as a matter of law, and in England as a matter of practice since the mid-'70s, a prosecution is not brought unless there is corroboration (i.e., some independent evidence tending to show that the accomplice is telling the truth). The Court of Appeal in England (in one of the cases which gave rise to the present English practice) criticised the fact that in one accomplice case ten accused were tried together. The court said this should not happen again. In the Black trial — the first major supergrass trial in Belfast — there were 38 people in the dock. About 20 of these were alleged by Black (who had been given immunity from prosecution on charges including murder and who, in common with many supergrasses, confessed to having lied on oath in a previous trial) to be members of the IRA; the rest were men and women, old and young, living in the New Lodge and Ardoyne areas of Belfast who were alleged to have allowed their houses to be used or to have in some way directly or indirectly, intentionally or otherwise assisted the IRA. The latter group were given non-custodial sentences (although almost all of them had remained in custody all during the eight-month trial); the former were to spend four years and four months in custody before being released by the Court of Appeal on the ground that Black's evidence was not capable of belief to the required standard.

Like the internees, all of them were suspected by the police, rightly or wrongly, of "terrorist" involvement. Similarly, those who allegedly made statements in Castlereagh or Gough may or may not have been guilty, but they were stripped of their rights and safeguards to such an extent that one could never be sure beyond reasonable doubt of the guilt of any accused in any contested statement case. Yet many of these people were sentenced to life imprisonment, and Michael Culbert and Raymond McCartney have now served ten and twelve years respectively.

When the British authorities or the old Stormont government interned people without trial, at least they were admitting that they were jailing them purely on suspicion. And they were effectively acknowledging that there was sufficient political support for those using violence against the institutions of the state to make it impossible to secure evidence against those involved. That is still the case today but they are reluctant to use internment now because they would have to derogate from the European Convention on Human Rights and would be admitting that there is a fundamental political problem in Northern Ireland which is no nearer resolution. They have, however, resisted all pleas to drop the power to intern from the Emergency Provisions Act. They are hedging their bets.

What is going on now is an exercise in deception whereby an appearance of normality is being fabricated. People are tried and charged under the law instead of being arbitrarily imprisoned, but the law and the courts have been adapted so that an accused person can be convicted and jailed without the police having to produce the type and quality of evidence that would be required in a "normal" common law jurisdiction. And there are also cases, of course, where there are indications that members of the police or British army have simply decided to kill persons they suspect of IRA involvement, but against whom they do not have sufficient evidence to secure a conviction even in the Diplock courts. Among the worst casualties of this practice of taking legal short cuts — apart of course from the victims of so-called shoot-to-kill incidents — are those who have been sentenced to life imprisonment on tainted evidence such as Castlereagh confessions and many of whom have now served twelve or 13 years in jail. Had these people been interned without trial the pressure for their release would have long since proved irresistible, but now to preserve the fiction that the law enforcement system is normal and regular and that they have been convicted and sentenced in the normal way, they must be forced to serve out their life sentences in full, having already served much longer than the average non-political murderer jailed after a jury trial in Britain. They are being sacrificed to the necessity of maintaining at all costs that it is not the state itself that has failed and is the cause of the problem.

The Northern Ireland state certainly cannot deliver the human rights demands that we started out by making 20 years ago. Everyone may now have a local government vote, but the local councils are in chaos as a result of the loyalist protests at the Anglo-Irish Agreement and their refusal to accept the presence of Sinn Féin councillors. Housing has improved, but can fair employment ever be implemented while loyalists still control the key industries and official reports acknowledge that the Fair Employment Act has had virtually no effect after twelve years? And we are a by-word around the world for repressive legislation, which not only does not solve the problem but is in itself a major contributor to the alienation of a whole section of the community. If I see one hopeful sign — and I hope I am not wrong — it is that some sections of loyalist opinion seem increasingly disenchanted with Britain. The crisis here *will* end some day and it will only be ended by talking. We should start that ourselves. After all we are all Paddies to our rulers in Stormont Castle.